the food lover's guide to the great ocean road

australia

This book is an initiative of Geelong Otway Tourism.

Published by
Hardie Grant Books
Private Bag 1600
South Yarra, Victoria 3141
Australia

First published in 1999
Revised in 2000

All rights reserved. No part of this publication may be reproduced, stored in a retrieval system or transmitted in any form by any means, electronic, mechanical, photocopying, recording or otherwise, without the prior written consent of the publishers and copyright holders.

Copyright © in text: Max Allen
Copyright © in images: Simon Griffiths

National Library of Australia
cataloguing-in-publication data:

Allen, Max, 1968 – .
    The food lover's guide to the Great Ocean Road:
    restaurants, wineries, people, places, produce, recipes

    Includes Index.

    ISBN 1 876719 65 6.

1. Restaurants – Victoria – Great Ocean Road – Guidebooks.
2. Wineries – Victoria – Great Ocean Road – Guidebooks.
3. Great Ocean Road – Guidebooks.
    I. Title

641.599457

Designed by Luisa Laino
Printed in Singapore by Tien Wah Press

MAX ALLEN

Max Allen is the author of *Red and White: Wine Made Simple*, which won the 1999 Andre Simon Memorial Award, one of the UK's most prestigious gongs for wine-scribbling. He is the wine columnist for *The Weekend Australian Magazine* and contributing editor for *Australian Gourmet Traveller's The Wine Magazine*. He also writes regularly for *House & Garden*, *Divine Magazine* and, in the UK, *WINE* magazine and *Decanter*. He writes the wine sections in the annual Australian 'Seasonal Produce Diary'. Max also runs popular wine education courses in Melbourne, where he lives (and occasionally gets to spend some time with) his wife, four-year-old daughter and new baby son.

SIMON GRIFFITHS

Simon Griffiths is a leading photographer of food, gardens and interiors. He created the stunning visuals for the best-selling *Stephanie Alexander and Maggie Beer's Tuscan Cookbook* and regularly travels overseas on assignments for *Gourmet Traveller* and *Vogue Living*. He has also collaborated with Paul Bangay on *The Defined Garden* and *The Boxed Garden*, and with Susan Irvine on *The Rose Gardens of the UK*.

GEORGE BIRON

George Biron and Diane Garrett live at Sunnybrae, Birregurra, where for the last ten years they ran their award-winning restaurant and cooking school. George has a passion for wild foods, and has presented at Masterclass on wild fungi and the Perigord black truffle with Dr Ian Hall. He is currently writing for *The Australian* and *The Age*, while continuing to develop teaching, kitchen and garden projects to add to the culinary collateral of the district.

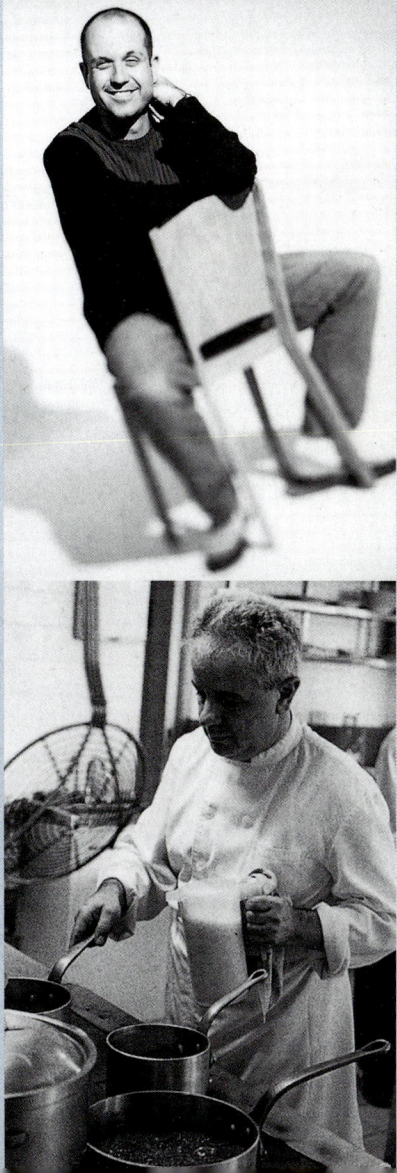

acknowledgements

Max Allen would like to thank the following people for their help putting this book together:

George Biron for opening his file and helping point me in the right direction and doing such a great job with his part of the book; Roger Grant of Geelong Otway Tourism for endless offers of lunch; Gail Thomas for sharing her knowledge and confirming my theories; the team at Hardie Grant for their confidence, persistence and tolerance; Simon Griffiths for driving and giving all those people who get bored with my words something stunning to look at; Luisa Laino making it all look so good; all the food and wine people along the Great Ocean Road who graciously opened jars, pulled corks, sliced hams, cut cheeses and served meals and talked and talked and talked; and most of all my family for putting up with the fact that I was away from home so much during the first quarter of this year.

Below • Fresh cheese at Timboon.

Right (top) • In the kitchen at Sempre, Geelong.

Right (bottom) • Snapper, Chris's at Beacon Point.

Over page • Lush farmland behind Apollo Bay.

contents

foreword	12
introduction	15
from the earth to the table	27
growers • producers • sellers • makers	
menu 1: a picnic on the barwon	47
blessed are the cheesemakers	51
menu 2: a family celebration	67
the grape treaders	71
vineyards • wines • winemakers	
menu 3: after the vintage	91
grand old days of queenscliff	95
menu 4: new year's eve at the turn of the century	107
kitchens and cooks	113
menu 5: at the restaurant	131
directory	134
recipe index	139
index	140
references and photo credits	142

foreword

There is a hidden danger in an innocent foray along the Great Ocean Road. It lies not in the curves along its scenic route, but rather in its beguiling beauty, in the majesty of the landscape and in the warmth and hospitality of the locals. Beware — it is catching.

My introduction to the area came in the heady days of the mid-seventies. We had just opened our first restaurant in Carlton and after an exhausting weekend I found myself in the back of a Mini-Moke, heading towards Lorne. That evening my mates took me to their local, a simple seaside restaurant. Around that table began friendships that have lasted for many years. This is a book about some of those people, as well as others who have made this district a haven for anyone with an appetite for clean, fresh flavours.

A cook always remembers the flavours. Towards the end of that evening our host joined us for some wine and, as cooks often do, we broke the ice by talking tucker. He taught me the difference between calamari and squid — in those days they were usually only used as bait. We talked about different types of fetta (he always used Bulgarian), of fresh fish and thick green olive oils. Soon the wine took over and I wandered off into the night, little knowing that ten years later I would be cooking the last meals in that kitchen where Christos Talihmanidis had began his saga; and that twenty years later, I would be harvesting artichokes from our country garden to serve with a very fine Victorian ewes' milk fetta, made by one of the descendants of those who first brought sheep to the district.

It was in this district that I learned the real meaning of hospitality. In the kitchens of the Queenscliff Hotel at the start of the eighties there was a real sense of the new. Patricia, Mietta and Robyn O'Donnell and Tony Knox had brought classic style to a sleepy seaside village. They had the vision. Now you can enjoy all the grand hotels and cafes, each with its own brand of Queenscliff cuisine. In those days most of the food had to be brought down from Melbourne. Waiters would run missions of mercy, but they would not return empty-handed, rushing the great local seafood back to their sister restaurant in town.

From the beginning, the hotel nurtured the idea of training for service. I can remember Philip Leahy and Ross Ebbels as cheeky schoolboys setting the fires (they are always set), and later as awkward 'commis'. Now, of course, they manage the hotel with the consummate style that Patricia has instilled into them.

I love foraging, be it for fungi, new ingredients or wine. Geelong is a great place to begin. At Neuschafers I have found remarkable aged rieslings in stelvin-capped bottles along with historic cases of Barossa Pearl!

If your interest lies in food memorabilia take a look into Mark Ward's amazing antique emporium. Browse the shelves of Barwon Books: their cooking section is second to none. For a beer with locals try the Sawyers Arms, where the Clatworthy family has dispensed good draught ale, fine food and wine for over forty years. Geelong is emerging from its industrial past as a vibrant waterfront city. Eastern Beach with its wide promenade holds a promise of things to come. The late John Wade and Graham Goldsworthy saw this potential more than two decades ago when Fishermen's Pier, or Fishos' as the locals call it, started to sell classy fish and chips overlooking the water. As the Deakin Architecture School develops and students from all over the world study there, the little warehouses, back lanes and shops will reflect the taste of the town. In fact, it's already started — check out Bazil's Foodstore.

The Great Ocean Road is a road to travel in all seasons. I love Lorne in the winter: woodfired pizza followed by a night at the Lorne Theatre, one of the most original art deco picture theatres in Victoria, a glimpse of old Lorne. It has its own film festival, 'Clickers', started over thirty years ago by Fred Schepisi and his mates. Bribe a local for an invite.

Autumn in Apollo Bay means seriously good coffee and a bite at the Bay Leaf Cafe, then back to the forest to bring back the fungi for the larder. But make sure you go with an expert!

For me, a country restaurant is a place where you can be made to feel at home in comfort, but most of all it should reflect its position and define its relationship with the environment. From the beginning, we were determined to be a showcase for the fine produce of the district. The region is steeped in tradition. I have spent cold winter days making traditional pork smallgoods with four generations of a local Italian farming family. We served local lowline beef bred for flavour and texture. Cindy (you will meet him later) hangs the local lamb and prepares the forcemeats for our home-made cotechinos. When I asked him if he could find the special casings he replied, 'Oh you mean the bungs — we used that for the strass years ago'.

Since the first edition of this book, new players have entered the scene like the wonderful sourdough bakery at Irrewarra — but sadly Sunnybrae has closed. After ten years, we have taken a new direction. We will continue to add to the culinary collateral of the district, but for now Sunnybrae will revert to being our home.

In this book, Max Allen takes you on a journey into our neck of the woods. Along with all the other people who work to make this district what it is, I welcome you to take that ride, as I was made welcome when I first arrived.

Simon Griffiths' magnificent photographs have captured the essence of the region. He is a joy to work with: no fuss, no umbrellas, just his lens and impish face quietly distilling and focussing the visual flavour of his subject.

Without producers like those Max has highlighted, our job would have been much harder. It has been a great pleasure to watch them develop their products, a privilege to taste the samples, and a joy to cook with them.

I would especially like to thank all of the people who supplied recipes for the book.

So take a ride with Max and his 'tummy'. But beware — you may, as I have, stay a little longer than you had planned.

George Biron.

George Biron
Sunnybrae, Birregurra

introduction

This is a food-lover's book about the Great Ocean Road, written by a food lover. (It's a wine-lover's book, too, although wine in this part of the world takes a back seat to food — for a change.) I think it's important to clarify this. Although plenty of books have been written about the Road before (and with good reason: it is spectacularly beautiful), nobody has taken the edible bits of the region and savoured them with quite as much single-minded relish.

This book certainly contains lots of beauty (mostly in the form of Simon Griffiths' gorgeous photographs), and it's simply not possible to write about the Road without being haunted, compelled and often quite daunted. But this book is, at the end of the day, mostly about putting good things in your mouth — and about the people and places that grow, make and cook those things.

That nobody has attempted a book like this before is not surprising. Despite being such a well-established part of the psyche of Victorians, Australians and the countless international visitors who travel along it each year, the Road itself is still a long way off celebrating its centenary. Indeed, some parts of it were not fully sealed until the middle of the 1980s. Tourism in general has only really taken off in a big, modern way right across the region in the last decade (although at resorts such as Queenscliff and Lorne, of course, it has been partying on for much longer).

But food — its production and consumption — has been a crucial part of the Great Ocean Road story since well before anybody thought that the Great Ocean Road might be a good idea, certainly aeons before the marketing boffins dreamed up the concept of promoting the food found along it. In some cases, food was a reason for opening up the coast of south-west Victoria; in most cases ensuring their family had food on the table was the first thing new settlers turned their minds to.

For the many rugged pioneers along the coast — the whalers at Port Fairy (then Belfast) and Warrnambool, the farmers at Apollo Bay, the early hoteliers at Lorne — the ocean itself, of course, has always been one seething, boiling fish stew. From tiny scallops and mussels, through simple wholesome fish such as schnapper, whiting, and the once-popular barracouta, to the regal and much-prized crayfish and abalone, Bass Strait has kept generations of locals fed since the early years of the nineteenth century. And despite almost two hundred years of, at times, intensive fishing activity, those who work these waters say that there is still plenty of food left.

The early settlers who opened up the western districts of Victoria turned the wide open granite country from Colac to Portland into one of Australia's most important areas for dairying. Cattle have grazed on the paddocks squeezed among the dry stone walls here for decades now, and their milk has found its way into untold mountains of butter, cheese and ice-cream.

Wool, too, has always been a major industry, with huge quantities of the soft stuff being shipped from Geelong to major export markets — in the same great steamers that carried those mountains of butter and cheese. And where there are sheep and cattle there is also beef and lamb: again, the western districts have long been known for the quality of their meat. Generations of Victorians here have been nourished by Sunday roasts — and Monday roasts, and Tuesday roasts ...

You have to eat some vegies occasionally, though, and farmers along the Road have always been willing to provide. From the black

Right • Hitchcock, Hendy and the men of the Great Ocean Road Trust, who were the instigators behind the building of the Road.

Previous page • The beach at Torquay, 1910.

volcanic country of the Bellarine Peninsula to the lush fertility of the Otways, every kind of traditional cooler-climate crop has been cultivated: onions, spuds, peas, herbs, berries, apples, root crops.

Almost as important with a roast and two veg is something refreshing to drink. And again, the people of the Great Ocean Road have been almost constantly supplied with grog since the very earliest days: both brewing and winemaking began in Geelong in a serious way as early as the 1840s, joined by distilling on a huge scale in the 1920s, with the renaissance of Geelong's vineyards in the 1960s joined by the beginnings of viticulture near Portland.

Most of these examples of primary food and drink production have developed in response to local demand. They were subsistence industries, designed, on the whole, to satisfy the hunger and thirst and create an income for the local population (the grand exception being the long-standing hotels and resorts, which by definition, are there to feed visitors, not just locals).

But, as I have said, in the last twenty years — and particularly in the last ten or even less — two new reasons have emerged for food and drink to be produced right across the region: tummy-led tourism and a burgeoning foodie awareness.

From the mid-1970s on, farmhouse cheese-makers started appearing, offering an alternative to the mountains of commercial yellow stuff. Wool producers started diversifying into wine and cheese and 'gourmet' meat. Enticing, modern cafes and

Left • Pick and shovel construction meant slow progress.

Above • Early holiday makers on the road to Lorne.

restaurants dispensing good food and wine with a smile started cropping up in places previously distinguished by their shallow tucker and sullen service. And individuals with vision started creating cottage industries for themselves by making high quality food and marketing it well — both within and without the region.

Food is now a primary reason for visiting the region. But it's worth looking back at how today's tummy-led tourism compares with the way food was viewed in the early years of the Great Ocean Road's establishment.

As far back as 1859, when the first telegraph line was run from Melbourne through Geelong, down to Cape Otway and across to Tasmania, settlement and food production were already well established in pockets along the coast.

George Clarke, a farmer at Eastern View, would load up his poor old pack pony with produce once a week — potatoes, huge sacks of peas — and navigate the treacherous track to Lorne, which was fast becoming a popular resort. People travelled overland from Winchelsea and Birregurra to the calm of Louttit Bay to dabble in a spot of fishing and walk in the dramatically spectacular bush.

On 30 December 1879, George Ernest 'Chinese' Morrison undertook a walk from Queenscliff to Adelaide (at the tender age of seventeen, mind you), navigating the same treacherous telegraph track as Clarke for much of the way. The story was published in a Melbourne newspaper, and food appears in glimpses, giving us a good idea of the tucker on offer at the time.

On setting off, Morrison's knapsack contained 'two loaves of bread, a well roasted boneless leg of mutton; half a pound of salt, ¼ lb, pepper; 3 lemons.' Yum. Oh, and a billy and some tea, of course. He got to Lorne in time for a New Year's dinner at Mountjoy's House, one of a couple of hotels standing proud among the vast cleared land (a pretty fair walk, when you think about it, even by today's bituminised standards).

The next day before he departed again he stocked up — or tried to: ' I had ordered a roast leg of mutton weighing 4lbs. Judge of my disgust when a boiled leg, weighing 9lbs made its appearance.' Yuck.

By the end of the century the idea of an Ocean Road between Geelong and Lorne was being popularly advocated — and debated — in the newspapers. The reasons for the Road were plentiful — with defence and simple accessibility obvious ones — but the scenic attractions and the opening up of western coastal Victoria to industries such as farming and, importantly, dairying were uppermost in the promoters' minds.

By 1918, a full head of steam had been achieved. Geelong's mayor, Howard Hitchcock, and a prominent councillor, E.E. Hendy, established the Great Ocean Road Trust, and embarked on a fund-raising drive across the region — part of which was the 'Great Ocean Road Cinema Picture', an ambitious documentary profile of the Road shot by film maker, C. R. Herschell (the film, including footage of the long-gone Apollo Bay Butter Factory, has tragically been lost — presumed destroyed).

Hitchcock and Hendy's angle was a winning one: the spectacular road to Lorne and beyond would not only honour those who had fallen in the Great War, but also provide employment for

many of those who returned — in fact, an early proposal had the road named as the 'Anzacs' Highway'.

According to a newspaper report from the period, life in the construction camps was anything but strenuous. A vegetable garden was planted near the main workers' camp at Lorne, 'and a variety of vegetables grow luxuriantly in the rich black soil. The men have their lunch brought to them by their cook, and a hot meal is ready for them when they return from work.'

Like many such reports, the writer here is infuriatingly short on foodie detail. What were the vegies? What did those lunches and hot meals consist of? Whatever, progress on the road was slow at the best of times and prone to stopping completely (fund-raising difficulties didn't help).

But by 1922, the first section of the Great Ocean Road from Geelong to Lorne was complete — in a fashion. On March 20, a fittingly grand motor cavalcade of dignitaries, including the Governor, Lord Stradbroke, made their slow and unsteady way to Lorne along the dusty track. Again, the celebratory dinner given at Erskine House that night was more memorable for its four hours (count 'em!) of speeches than for its food, but interestingly, we do know that only orange juice was served.

By the time the Road was completed to Warrnambool in 1932, however, there was much more than just orange juice being doled out along its length. At the resorts of Queenscliff, Torquay, Anglesea and Lorne, and in hotels that had sprung up with other newer settlements along the Road, a thriving trade in all manner of things alcoholic had been established. Eastern View, for example, now had a proper hotel which, in the 1930s, had the rather incredible reputation for stocking any drink the customer could name.

Left • George Ernest 'Chinese' Morrison, who walked from Queenscliff to Adelaide at age 17.

Above • Geelong, c.1905.

By the 1960s, the Road's former glory and allure had faded a little: resorts continued to attract the crowds during summer, but no new influx or interest had arrived. Then the surf culture began to blossom on the beaches at Torquay, and Lorne and surrounds became a destination for artists and other Melbourne city-types anxious to escape the big smoke.

The Road has suffered many natural disasters: landslides, flooding and the Ash Wednesday fires in 1983. But it has survived to see its former glory return. Since the 1980s, a steadily increasing stream of people have travelled the Road, keen to visit the resorts, the natural wonders of the region — rainforests, the Sow and Piglets (the original, and I think far better name for the Twelve Apostles) and the whales — as well as the unnatural wonders: shipwrecks, lighthouses, old buildings.

And now, at the turn of the millennium, more and more people are journeying down the Road to eat and drink.

This book is the story of my personal eating and drinking journey. In some ways, it is a food-lover's guide, written not by one who loves food but by one who is food-obsessed. I am fascinated by food, and by what gets my saliva flowing and my tummy rumbling.

Other people's memories mostly revolve around images. I have a cloud of smells and a tangle of tastes writhing around on the edge of my brain. Where other people reconstruct their experiences by recalling who they met, what they did and what music they were listening to, I'll bring back recollections of who I ate with, how the potatoes were cooked and what vintage of so-and-so's pinot noir we were drinking. I perceive life through eating and drinking.

Sometimes, this exclusive tummy-oriented perception can be quite a burden, let me tell you. For example, while everybody else is gazing through the car window admiring the spectacular towering trees that line the side of the Road as it runs through the Otways, I'm half-way out the door taking in lungfuls of the blackcurrant-and-mint smells pouring off the gums.

Hurtling into Port Campbell, the sea to the left, a startling blue sky above, the wide brown flat lands stretching away to the right, all I can think of is how the roaring surf sounds uncannily like a cappuccino machine (a thought triggered, possibly, by the fact that we are so far from the safe cappuccino culture of Melbourne).

And at various points along the Road, as it snakes away from the sea and takes the driver inland, through pastures, small towns and clumps of straggly bush, a sign keeps popping up which never fails to make me smile and drift off into a hungry, pre-lunch reverie (I get to be the passenger a lot, luckily). 'Give Way To Stock' says the sign, innocently, and all I can picture is the heavenly smell of a huge pot of simmering beef bones (Western District beef, of course), destined for consomme and the juices of a stew, and the sticky richness of a reduced sauce.

There are personal food memories, too, that date back to way before I started writing this book. Roast chicken and a local cabernet in the gentle calm of Port Fairy's Merrijig Inn one summer evening; drinking pinot noir and eating frankfurters in a shack in the middle of Bannockburn vineyard; taking excited children blackberry-picking in a wild forest behind Apollo Bay in early autumn; fish and chips and a cold, cold pot in Lorne.

Left • Seventies surfari at Point Lonsdale.

I have travelled the Road from Lara to Portland and headed off inland as far as the Princes Highway, Colac and Camperdown (we had to draw the line somewhere). I have spent a lot of time tasting, eating, talking, drinking. I was looking for good food and wine, yes, but I was also looking for other people with passion, people whose stories inspired me, people who made me want to eat better, drink better, live better.

This is not an exhaustive look at all the food and wine along the Great Ocean Road. It contains lots of thoroughly personal perceptions, as well as critical appraisal and subjective choice. Like any portrait, it is selective (and, like any portrait, it may not always please all of the subjects all of the time). I have simply searched for and written about those people who sum up what is haunting, compelling and delicious about this spectacular part of the world.

introduction 25

from the earth to the table

growers • producers • sellers • makers

If there is once piece of essential advice I would give to food-lovers travelling along the Great Ocean Road it would be this: take a large Esky.

The region is dotted with people who are growing things, processing things, smoking things, cooking things, preserving things, fermenting things and selling things to eat. Many is the time that you will find yourself tempted by roadside signs offering fruit, eggs, vegies, cheese, cakes, smallgoods, bread, wine ... Take an Esky and you won't be nagged for the rest of your holiday by that vague feeling you might have missed out on something sensational.

While on the surface the Great Ocean Road is not the first place you might think of when it comes to discussing Australia's great food regions, there is no doubt that there is plenty of great food stuff happening there. The Barossa in South Australia may have a longer, more focussed tradition of mettwurst and German wine festivals and long-established grape-growing families. North-east Victoria may have a more concentrated tradition of ethnic Italian migrant food culture. But the Great Ocean Road is no less blessed by good people doing good things — it's just that these people are scattered and often hidden, and it is harder to pin them all down at once.

They are people down a dusty road that runs behind the main drag in town, making food in their front rooms. People who don't open to the public, and sell only through a small number of outlets. People tucked away in the moist green folds of the Otway Ranges. People who, on the surface, may not look like committed food producers at all.

Dairying has a long and visible history in this part of the world. Meat production and fishing, too, have been viable industries for well over a century. And wine has a stop-start history stretching back a hundred and fifty years. But I'm talking about a newer food culture than that — a food culture along the Great Ocean Road that is young and fragile. Small producers hand-crafting food. Passionate practitioners of traditional methods and philosophies. People committed to the highest quality on a small scale. People looking to express some sense of place through what they grow or make or cook.

These new food producers are not always all that vocal or adept at marketing themselves. Some of the best food and wine people don't even know some of the others exist. And some of the best producers are better known in Sydney than they are in their neighbouring town — which says as much about the youthful nature of the food-consuming culture here as the culture of food production.

If the new food culture is youthful, the idea of an identifiable regional cuisine is barely a twinkle in the eye of one or two visionary chefs and producers. As yet, there is not a strong enough network of suppliers and not enough people willing to pay that little bit extra for local, small-production food. George Biron has created regional menus in this book, but they are more a celebration of some great ingredients that are produced locally and seasonally, than a reflection of any long-standing food tradition (although there are elements expressed of those traditions that do exist).

But the big point is this: there is nothing wrong with having a young and fragile food culture. Regionalism may be a buzz-word in the food and wine worlds at the moment, but the Great Ocean Road is such a vast area, and the many food cultures that exist along it are so diverse, that the best we can say is this: within this wide and sprawling region, there are indeed people producing great food.

Top • Angel Cardoso, the King of Ham.
Bottom • Jamon in the curing room.
Previous page • The beach at Apollo Bay.

The King of Ham

Fat. Such a small word, yet so stuffed with connotation. For too many people in our greedy, over-indulged society, this little word has become a source of fear and loathing — something to be avoided at all costs if you want to be 'healthy'.

For Angel Cardoso, fat is something to be embraced and given a big sloppy kiss. Because Angel's incredibly good smallgoods — hams, chorizos, sausages, salamis — simply wouldn't have that other-worldly flavour that sends foodies crazy with desire if it weren't for their generous marblings of fat (the smallgoods, not the foodies).

Forgive me. I'm raving, I know. But I have a very soft spot for the food (and wine) of Spain. And I have a particularly tender spot for the glorious, silken, complex allure of a good jamon, the Iberian equivalent of Italy's prosciutto.

I fell deeply in love with jamon on a food and wine journalist's junket across Spain a couple of years ago (hard life, yes, I know). Paper-thin slices carved from huge legs in tapas bars: translucent ruby, glistening, nutty-smelling, melt-in-the-mouth textured and impossibly rich in flavour.

So imagine my ecstatic surprise when, on returning, I discover this passionate Spaniard making jamon in Lara, of all places, just outside Geelong. No ordinary jamon, either: jamon as good as some of the best I tasted in his homeland.

Angel Cardoso knows how good his products are. It's a source of great pride to him. Sitting at his kitchen table, hunk of bread in one hand, glass of rich Spanish red wine in the other, he swells up like a balloon and his eyes widen when he relates the praise that has been poured on him by respected food people such as Stephanie Alexander, Cherry Ripe and George Biron.

He's got every right in the world to be proud: he reckons it took him close to twenty years and tens of thousands of dollars in wasted meat trying to perfect the 'recipe' for his jamon. Two decades to achieve near-perfection. That's passion.

Angel was born in verdant Galicia, on Spain's northern coast, sixty-five years ago. He grew up in Madrid and arrived in Australia in 1962 on his twenty-eighth birthday. When he arrived, he says, he found there was so much in Australia — so much great produce, quality meat, potential — but nobody was doing anything with it. So he decided to. He had come to work in the aeronautical industry but began experimenting with jamon in spare rooms.

Eventually he ended up in Lara, a broad, low, country town with a good view across dusty paddocks to the You Yangs rising from the earth. Here in 1973 he had the opportunity to get serious, and he built a two-storey house: upstairs — bright and very Spanish — for his family; and downstairs — dark and cellar-like — for his ham.

As soon as Angel opens the heavy wrought-iron screen door to his house, the smell of ham — and the sausage and the salami — billows out in delicious sweet clouds from these cool dark cellars. A smell of pimento, so essential for the orange-red colouring and piquancy of the chorizo; of garlic, so essential for binding the meat; of tender salty pork; and something more elusive, more earthy, like mushrooms — *setas* in Spanish. It's the smell of the beneficial and harmless grey mould that settles on the outside of Angel's smallgoods as they hang, curing, for six to nine months in the case of the jamon, only perhaps two in the case of the *lomo*, or cured loin of pork.

This is the one part of this story that we can put down more to luck than passionate hard work. As soon as Angel began hanging his smallgoods in the dark cellars under his house over two decades ago, opening fly-screened windows every now and then to let the winds from the Lara plains dry his meat, this mould began to appear. And far from spoiling the meat, it actually contributes a complexity and depth of flavour. So he was lucky with his mould: what took him far longer to pin down was the way he applied the salt during the curing process, and getting the meat control right.

'Not many people have the patience to do this,' he says, gulping down some more red wine. 'But if you don't push for these things there is no future — only the pie and the pastie. A lot of people are just trying to make money, but their brains are being destroyed. My mother used to tell me 'forget about money — the money's in your brain'. So I make a living, I have enough. But I am more proud of what I have done, and what I am doing for this country. I was not born in Australia but that doesn't matter. I'm here now. This is my life.'

I take a paper-thin slice of jamon, a slice of Angel's life. It smells sweet and tempting, like hazelnuts and warm afternoons. The flesh is a glowing red, the fat coloured like an apricot rose. You know the jamon is ready when the fat has this colour. I fold the slice into my mouth. The flesh melts, its silky texture touching every corner of the tongue. But it's the fat that holds the flavour — deep, salty, satisfying.

Luckily, finding Angel's glorious smallgoods is a little easier now than it was until quite recently. For a long time, most of what he made was consumed by Australia's fairly sizeable Spanish community — much of it going through the Casa Iberica retail and distribution business (Angel is godfather of the Casa Iberica daughters). But in the last couple of years, the foodie set have discovered Angel Cardoso, and today you'll not only see his jamon and chorizo appearing regularly at Cafe Botticelli, Geelong and Sunnybrae Restaurant at Birregurra (where it has been for years) but also on trendy menus in Melbourne and further afield.

If you do find it, try it. And discover that in this case, fat is nothing to be afraid of. It is a thing of beauty and a joy forever.

The deli trail

There's shopping and there's shopping. For me, shopping for clothes has to be one of the most unexciting activities in the world. (Less diplomatic friends would say that this was pretty obvious.) On the other hand, I could spend all day shopping for food or wine. Poring over jars of oil; picking through cartons of apples; sniffing cheeses; admiring fish. Makes me hungry just thinking about it.

Great Ocean Travellers are fairly well catered for by green grocers and delis. In Warrnambool, Pud's Pantry stocks a fine range of deli items as well as selling its own, nicely rustic breads and pastries. In Lorne, the ticklishly named Lorne Greens (Bonanza, yes, but does anybody remember Battlestar Galactica?) is just next to the Marine Cafe, and is a slice of city fruiterer-chic: French sea salt, Italian parmesan, quinces and spiced Indian Tea sit next to local cheeses and organic produce.

But the biggest concentration of food stockists, of course, is Geelong. Mondo Deli in Pakington Street sells a wide and tempting range of local produce, from cheese to ham to bacon. Hero Deli in Little Malop Street is more European in character, and specialises in home-made Polish-style sausages.

But my favourite is V & R, at the top end of Pakington Street. Run by Vince and Rosa Gangemi, this wholesale and retail business operates out of a warehouse-type building, but has a very human scale to it. Presentation is not slick but honest, simple and very tempting, with a wonderful range of fruit and veg of very high quality on offer.

Fridges are stuffed with local produce, from cheese to bacon, as well as the best from elsewhere — South Australian olives, Italian oil, etc. Breads include the powerfully flavoured range of sourdough and olive-flavoured examples from the Mediterranean Bread Company in Moorabool Street.

If you're heading down the Road and need to stock up for a picnic, stopping here would be a great idea.

Left • Hero Deli, Little Malop St, Geelong.

The sound of one loaf baking

The name Zen does not immediately conjure up pictures of Italian master bakers and crusty, rustic pasta dura loaves and olive rolls. But it will by the time you get to the end of the next paragraph.

Danny Zen and his family run the Zen Artisan Cafe Bakery on a busy shopping strip in Belmont, South Geelong. The bakery has been in the family for fifteen years. Danny's parents, Gianni and Albina travelled to Australia from the Veneto in the 1950s. Gianni was a master baker, and when they started in Belmont, pasta dura — a hard, traditional crusty style of sourdough loaf, with fluffy soft insides — was but one of many breads produced, along with doughnuts, hedgehogs, viennas, vanilla slices.

The regular passing trade at the time wasn't particularly interested in pasta dura, although the local Italians loved it — especially after a few days, when the loaf becomes even crustier, better for mopping up soup and sauce. But according to Danny Zen, the last few years have seen some big changes.

For a start, chains such as Brumby's have lifted the game presentation-wise. So the Zen Artisan Cafe Bakery did too. It's now a cafe, brightly painted, Frank Sinatra on the stereo, fresh flowers on the tables. But more importantly, the local clientele changed. They suddenly wanted pasta dura. They even liked it very crusty.

Zen was overjoyed. So he tried something new. He tracked down the best recipe for ciabatta he could find (from a baker in Italy, via the Internet), and tested the water. It was a success (and tasting it you can see why: light, airy, yeasty, but still with just enough chew). He has also seen a change among the wholesale clients he supplies. Restaurants are seeking him out for his traditional Italian bread (Kosta's in Lorne has his ciabatta, for example) and, best news of all, local restaurants are beginning to move away from price-based purchasing towards buying on quality.

Now that is something worth meditating on.

Have your cake and eat it too

I will never forget the sight of two rather big and butch working men standing at the counter in the tiny, cramped Freshwater Creek Cake Shop, stocking up on delicate pink butterfly cakes, and chocolate eclairs, and jam tarts. I will also never forget the image that flashed through my mind of the same two blokes pulling their truck over suddenly somewhere further down the Anglesea Road, unable to contain themselves any longer — gorging themselves on the sweet fancies until they were sick, washing each morsel down with weak but scalding hot coffee sucked from polystyrene cups.

Then again, I can understand the impulse. Simon and I stocked up too when we were last passing (you can't miss the shop; Freshwater Creek ain't exactly a bustling metropolis). We filled a box (we'd forgotten the Esky) with excellent home-made Anzacs, as well as Gentle Annie's superb silvanberry jam from Pennyroyal Farm, one of the region's best pick-your-owns at Deans Marsh, as well as local honey and bags of apples and pears plucked that very morning from trees just across the road from the shop. And a couple of those pink butterfly cakes (which were scrummy). And an eclair. Talk about a regional showcase.

Oh, all right, so there was a whole passionfruit sponge as well. But we didn't eat it all at once. Honest.

from the earth to the table

Screaming Seeds

Some lessons you learn the hard way.

Albie Cachia had opened little sample pots of all her spice mixes for me to smell. I'd known about her successful company, Screaming Seeds, for years, and had tried individual mixes before, but this was a great opportunity to try the whole range, sitting in the shade of the factory where they were made, as fresh as they come.

As each pot was opened and passed to me, my excitement levels rose. The pungent, heady aromatic perfume of the garam masala; the incredibly scented and evocative Virgin Island Mix; the sweet warmth and fruity complexity of the Southern Cajun mix; the earthy, toasted, smoky notes of the dukkah.

Albie says that the extraordinary smells of her spice mixes take some women to the verge of orgasm. I believe her. I was getting a little giddy myself. My nostrils were in raptures, my olfactory bulb was throbbing with pleasure, my head was swimming. While Simon took Albie off to have her photo taken, I lunged for the next pot, ripped the top off and accidentally sucked up a nose-full. Literally.

And thus began the lesson. Inhaling Screaming Seeds' Kashmiri Krush mix is not to be recommended. Although it is not the hottest of the mixes (Caribbean Chilli holds that honour) it

Left • V&R Fruit and Vegetable Market, Geelong.

Above • A spicy mix at Screaming Seeds.

still contains a fair whack of ground-up pointy red peppers. And capsaicin, the substance that gives chillies their heat, is particularly vicious when it comes into contact with delicate nasal membranes.

You get the picture: I was in agony. But somehow, it was still pleasurable.

Screaming Seeds is one of the most successful small food producers in the region. Five years ago, Albie was working in restaurants and had this idea to develop a range of seasonings. Today, eighty kilos of spices go out to a huge number of outlets across Victoria and other states each week as well as to New Zealand and the UK. The day we were there, Albie had just made a contact in the Northern Territory — who in turn was talking of export to Hong Kong.

Then again, the company deserves to be a huge success. The packaging is great and Albie and her small team are tireless promoters, travelling thousands of kilometres each year attending food festivals, exhibitions and tastings. Information is the key here — as in providing as much of it as possible to the consumer in the form of tips, recipes, inspiration. A cookbook is being planned, with recipes contributed by Albie's favourite chefs.

But as I've already hinted, the spice mixes themselves are the real reason for people going crazy about Screaming Seeds — they really are fabulous. Which is why visiting the place where they are made is such a delicious revelation. I used the word 'factory' before just to throw you off the scent. Screaming Seeds spice mixes are actually roasted, blended and packed in a small converted bungalow on the outskirts of the sleepy town of Bellbrae.

The living-room is the packing room, office, store, brainstorming nerve centre. And the dizzily fragrant, tiny converted kitchen is the roasting room. A small domestic electric oven is all there is here for spice roasting. On all day. In goes one pan, out comes another. A selection of three grinders — two of which are your common or garden variety — have pride of place by the window. Cans of whole spices are arranged on shelves. That's about it, really. But this simplicity is deceptive. Whole spices are necessary, to preserve freshness and quality — as is roasting and blending on a small scale.

For the last three years, this kitchen has been home to Gerard McGill, an artist who divides his time between here and an old converted service station next door. Gerard is the roaster and blender. I asked him if he ever got sick of being exposed to the incredibly pungent smells his work entailed.

'Oh no,' he said, smiling. 'I love them. Especially cardamom. I always feel a lot healthier after I've been roasting cardamom.'

And in this case, children, that's one trick you can try at home.

Carackers at The Biscuit Tin

Between them, Karin Leahy and Esther Smits have seven children from the ages of five to eleven. That, you would think, even with the most understanding and helpful partners in the world, would be enough for most people.

But oh no. Karin and Esther have, for the last two and a half years, also been running an increasingly successful company, called The Biscuit Tin, from the front room of a small house down a sleepy road in Drysdale on the Bellarine Peninsula. A mini-production line of what look like waffle-toasters takes pride of place in the centre of the room. The smell of fresh butter and rich cheese and warm pepper sits thickly in the air. From these toasters comes a steady stream of Swiss-style Brezeli crackers (packaged as Carackers): wafer thin, crisp savoury biscuits that are, depending on your point of view, great with cheese, or great with a good cold lager (the poppyseed-studded ones are also lovely with spicy young red wine).

There are many brands of these rough-edged wafery crackers on the market, but the Carackers are the best — they use all-natural ingredients, from good butter to freshly ground pepper, and good grated cheese. As a consequence, prices are a little higher, but if you want quality, you have to be prepared to pay.

Karin came to Australia from Switzerland fourteen years ago. She had done her cooking apprenticeship there, and in this country worked in various kitchens on the Peninsula, becoming known for her cakes and crackers. She met Esther through their kids' school, and they decided to make a go of producing the crackers commercially.

They took up a sample package to a food fair in Melbourne — and were swamped with orders. 'We did everything the wrong way round,' says Karin. 'We had the product, we had the sales, then we had to do the small-management course and get the packaging right.'

Now they have distribution in four states, and they are looking at importing a bigger, automatic machine. While the quality of the ingredients will not change, the shape will: the distinctive rough-edged character of the carackers comes from the fairly haphazard waffle-iron toasters, and an automatic machine will ensure even edges. Which in some ways is a shame, but only a very, very tiny one.

The Birregurra Butcher

They don't make butchers like Cindy any more. In a world dominated by paranoid health regulations, hygiene, and bureaucracy, Cindy the butcher at Birregurra, near Colac, seems like a blast from the past. (Solid, nuggetty blokes who work with very sharp knives don't tend to get called Cindy any more, either, but Cindy's been Cindy for most of his life — even his bank manager calls him by his nickname.)

It's not that Cindy's butchery is anything but hygienic. It's just that the flyscreened-off work

How to make a sourdough starter

Niko Lewis, Babka, Fitzroy

Boil 3 medium potatoes until quite soft, puree and mix with 3 cups of cold boiled water. Add 2 cups of wholemeal rye flour. Adjust consistency with cold boiled water to make a medium thick slurry. Place in a glass jar that is twice the volume of the batter. Cover with a cloth and store at room temperature for about 3 days. The mix will start to bubble. When it has risen place into a larger container and add another 3 cups of the rye flour and 3 cups of water. Leave for at least 12 hours in a warm place. When it has started to bubble again it is ready to use.

area, nearly forty-year-old butcher's block (a rift valley worn in the middle of the wood) and creaking old building (eighty-seven years in the same business) don't look all that ... well, modern. Until just a few weeks ago there was even sawdust on the floor here, but they finally made him get rid of it.

They'll have a harder job with the Collingwood paraphernalia plastered all over the walls. Cindy is a mad Magpies fan; where most modern butchers have glossy photos of new trim lamb, Cindy has the black and whites. Then again, there is no chilled display cabinet here, either. The only meat you'll see from your side of the fly screen is what Cindy is chopping on the block — everything else is kept in a cool room out the back.

What Cindy has in his cool room is a great display of what the western districts do best: good lamb, not too fat, and great beef, bought and aged by Cindy — Hereford, Angus. He cut me a huge slice of rump and I had trouble remembering the last time I had beef that good from a Melbourne butcher. Cindy also says there's a bloke out near him trialing the much-prized Wagyu beef cattle. Could be a good business in the future.

In the meantime, Cindy will just keep on turning out great steak and burgers and sausages. 'I've been here for forty-three years,' he says. 'Sometimes I want to piss off, but I couldn't do anything else. So I reckon I'll just stay here for a while longer.'

Sticky Fingers

I first went to Sticky Fingers a couple of years ago. My wife was working on a story about the honey-lover's haven tucked down a side road in Aireys Inlet, so we all piled into the car (both of us and our baby daughter) and drove down there one beautiful day.

Graham and Charlene Angus had set up Sticky Fingers as a cafe and shop about three years prior to that visit, and were establishing a reputation for great honey. When we got there we weren't disappointed. In the small shop with its great welcoming sign (painted by Jeff Raglus, a local artist whose work will be familiar to Mambo-wearers) we discovered the pleasure of delicate wildflower honey; the heady perfume of rich blue gum-honey; the joy of real, white creamed honey; and the almost painfully intense powerhouse of flavour that is good stringy-bark honey.

Graham Angus also took us for a walk down the road to have a look at a few hives that were gathering some of the local wildflowers (so fragile and easily trodden underfoot) and did the very impressive playing with bees without being stung trick that apiarists seem to enjoy so much. And when we got back to the cafe, we gorged on sensationally rich Russian honey cake and sipped a honey liqueur made by a Melbourne honey fanatic, while Graham extolled the virtues of pollen (as in consuming it in its raw state) for anybody with allergies such as hayfever. I wasn't convinced — I'd rather have my pollen in its processed form, thank you very much.

Charlene and Graham are no longer together in a personal sense, but Graham still makes and sells honey through the shop Charlene still runs. She still makes her sensationally rich Russian honey cake and ginger balls, but she has added other strings to her bow: baklava is now a regular feature, and sourdough and fruit loaves are baked on the premises. Sticky Fingers also now does catering.

And Charlene's now promoting the virtues of pollen..

Right: Sticky Fingers welcome sign painted by Mambo's Jeff Raglus.

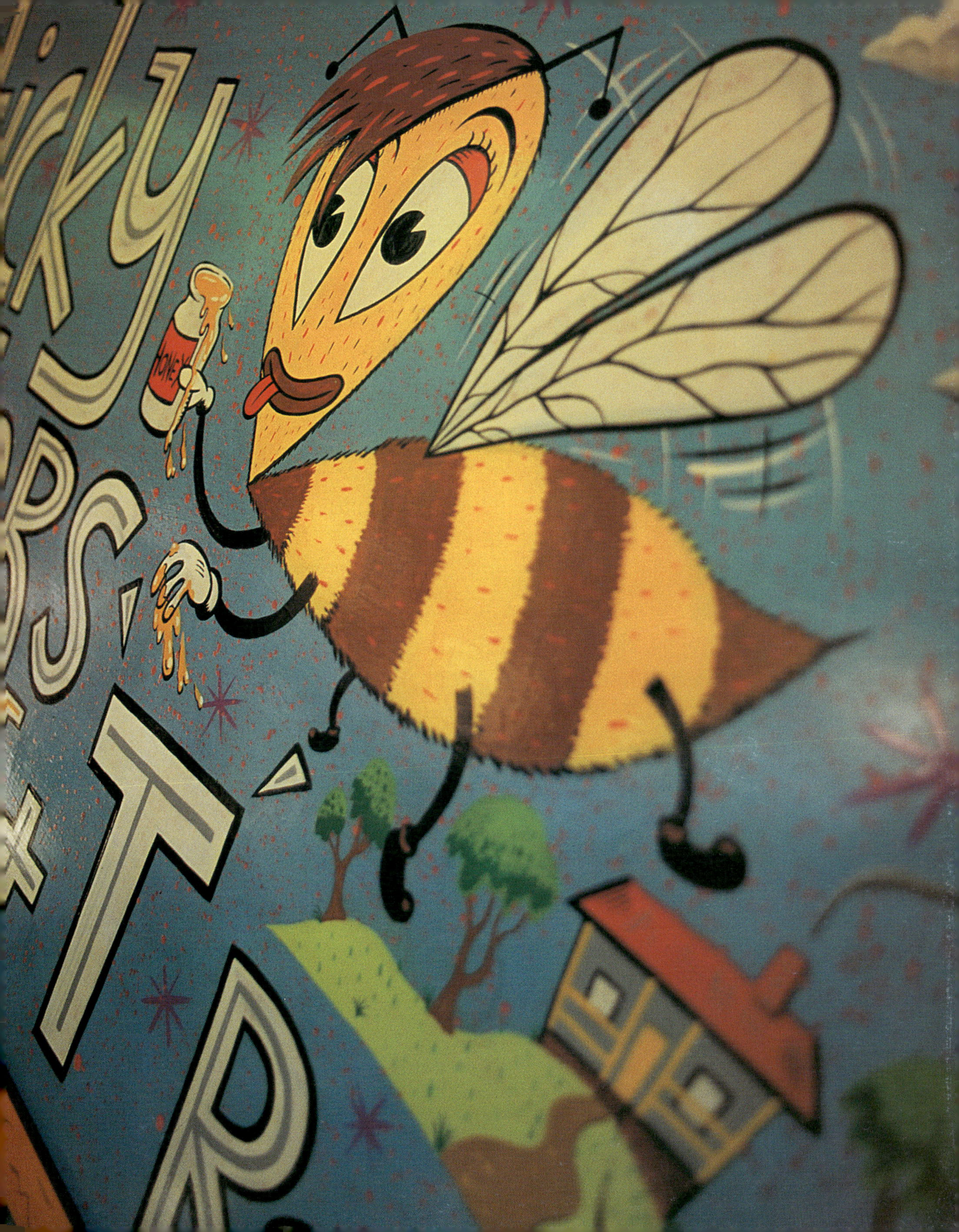

How to cook a cray

A cray under 2 kg is a waste of time. It must be alive. You will need a large pot and a heat source strong enough to sustain a good rolling boil. Drown the cray in icy cold fresh water — this will take about four hours. Fill the pot with half fresh and half seawater, or use good sea salt. Don't be mean — it has to be salty. Bring the water to the boil, add the cray and time it from when the water comes back to the boil (use your lid). Six minutes per kilo and six for the pot. Remove the cray and cool it down, but not in cold water. This will only make it soggy, a favourite trick of some fishmongers. In a plastic bag on ice is excellent. When ready, cut it in half remove the intestinal tract, pound the coral with 2 cloves of garlic and a teaspoon of Dijon mustard, slowly adding fine olive oil to make a thick homogenous paste. Add the juice of a lemon, salt and pepper. Eat it in friendship with a green salad and a cold ale.

Above • Stewart Atchison of Fishermen's Pier.

Cobden Country-Style Smokehouse

I was a vegetarian once. For a while. And like many other lapsed vegos, my nemesis came in the form of a lustily scoffed bacon sandwich (there was also that incident with the kebab, but we don't have to go into that right now). The bacon wasn't from Cobden Country-Style Smokehouse, but I wish it had been: my fall from grace would have been even more sinfully delicious.

Cobden bacon is developing a fairly strong following both locally, along the Road, in Geelong and also in Melbourne, where it is sold through such swanky outlets as the Richmond Hill Cafe and Larder. The company is owned by Alan Bellman, a Cobden butcher who started building a range of German-style smallgoods in the early 1990s. A couple of years ago Bellman also opened a restaurant and deli to sell his wares in the old Tandarook Cheese factory (built 1895) just south of Cobden. The restaurant is fairly basic and notable more for its great sense of history, wonderful old photographs and open, country-style kitchen than for its food. Not all the Cobden products impress me, either (although friends swear by two I wasn't able to try due to seasonality — the smoked duck and turkey) but the bacon is undoubtedly brilliant. Full-flavoured, sweet and hammy without being unduly porky, and with generous streakings of good fat (there's that word again), it cries out to be piled into the largest frying pan you can find, cooked until crispy, wedged between two doorstops of soft white bread, and wolfed down with a mug of strong, hot milky tea, on a crisp Ocean Road morning.

Enough to weaken the hardest vegetarian's resolve, I would have thought.

The fisher folk

Here's a tip from Nick Polgeest, Apollo Bay resident for thirty-five years and director of the town's fishing co-op. If you ever find yourself staying in his part of the world in self-catered accommodation (of which there is plenty — including the Colonial Cottages that Polgeest runs) and get bored of the twenty or so eateries in town (God forbid), head up to the co-op's shop on Breakwater Road and buy yourself some barracouta. Don't be put off by the fish's less-than-pretty appearance, and be patient with the bones. Persist, and make fishcakes, for they will be the best fishcakes you will ever eat.

Polgeest should know. At the age of twenty-one he was running a fish and chip shop in Colac, and he was making fishcakes out of couta then. Not long after, he started working on the fishing boats in Apollo Bay, when couta was the main catch — up to twenty boxes a day for each boat, depending on the market demand (which was then high).

In the early 1970s, a market for crayfish emerged, and the noble crustacea took over as Apollo Bay's main haul. Then tastes changed as the deep sea fishing industry grew. People wanted filleted fish, boneless, easy — and suddenly they didn't want a bar of couta (sorry, but it was Polgeest's pun, not mine). Luckily, export markets began to hear about the quality of Apollo Bay cray, and about fifteen years ago the sale of the beasts — live — to Beijing and Shanghai (where they like their crays banquet-sized) began to grow.

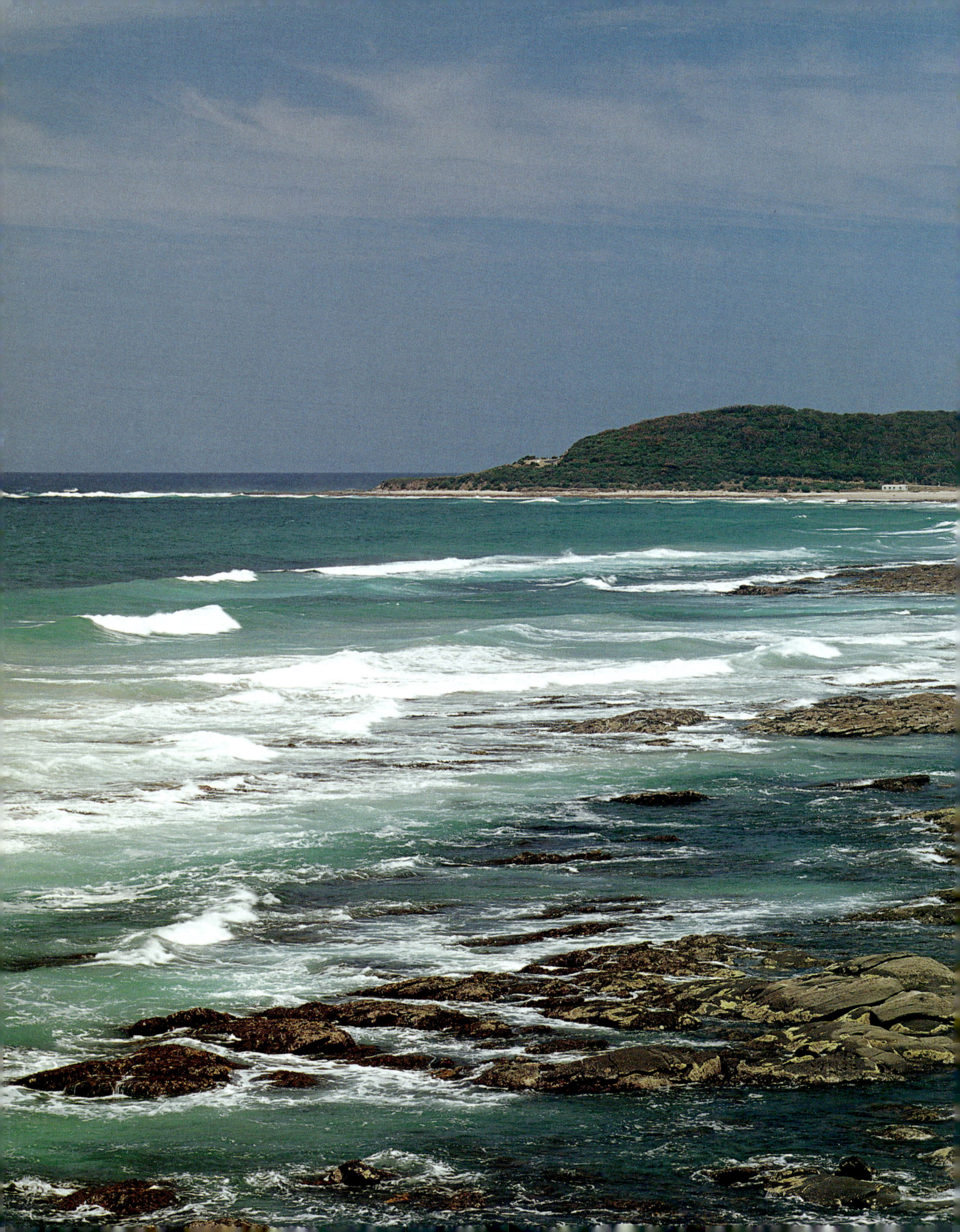

from the earth to the table

Today, Polgeest describes that export market as Apollo Bay's saving grace. They still fish for shark and a little squid here, and some cray go through the co-op shop, but it's the tonnes of squirming crustacea that are sent overseas that really provide a living for the people who run the Bay's twelve cray boats.

Cray is not the only export. Polgeest is also involved with a group who farm eels in Lake Colac for export, to Germany mostly, where they are a much-loved delicacy (unlike Australia, where they are viewed on the whole as little better than worms that swim).

But it's another big export industry that pulls in the real dollars: abalone. Again, visitors to the co-op shops in places such as Apollo Bay and Port Fairy can purchase this noble shellfish over the counter, but such sales are but a tiny fraction of those made overseas each year. There are about seventy licensed abalone divers in Victoria, and when you think that a single diving licence can be worth $1 million, you begin to get a picture of how valuable abalone is — especially considering that the Tasmanian ab industry is twice Victoria's size. Thirty-seven of those Victorian divers are found in the central zone of the state — along the Great Ocean Road, in other words.

One of them is Joel Shannon, who has been an ab diver in Apollo Bay for thirty years (which is also about how long the industry has been going). He remembers how the image of abalone has changed. In the late 1960s Shannon was lucky to get twenty cents a pound for abalone, once described by Hemingway as 'mutton fish'. Today it is such a desirable delicacy in many Asian countries that $1000 per kilo is not uncommon on the black market.

I have to admit here that try as I might, I still can't see the attraction of this fish. The word rubbery springs to mind rather too easily, although I'm quite willing to concede I may have simply been unlucky. Joel Shannon, however, used to be a chef, and has a recipe that makes my mouth water.

'Take a whole abalone and pound it: the fresher it is, the less you have to pound it. Fry the thing whole, briefly, then slice, sprinkle with lemon juice and some of the extremely good abalone sauce made by Lonimar, a processor in Kensington, Melbourne.'

So, now you know.

Further round the coast, towards Melbourne, abalone and cray are still important, but other fish and crustacea begin to figure as prominently.

Stand on the high crest of the Bellarine Peninsula on a clear sunny day and look north towards the You Yangs and the shimmering sea is studded with lines of mussel ropes. Lance Wiffen runs a mussel farming business called Sea Bounty. He farms mussels in Westernport Bay and Port Phillip, and says that the latter are plumper, sweeter, for a longer chunk of the year.

Until about five years ago, Wiffen fished for scallops, but when that activity was banned by the Victorian government, Wiffen moved to mussels. He now sells up to 600 tonnes of the live bivalves each year, and says that demand (from both restaurants and retail) has increased dramatically in that time. He then switches into hard-sell mode.

'Eating trends have changed,' he enthuses. 'Cookbooks and cooking shows have made people more confident. They are also becoming aware of the benefits of mussels. They are incredibly high in protein: as high as — but with a lower fat content — than steak. And they have the highest level of omega-3 fatty acids of all fish, but one. And there is an anti-arthritic quality to mussels ... '

He needn't have bothered. Unlike abalone, I'm already in love with mussels. But I think I love King George whiting more (simply dusted with seasoned flour, quickly panfried, squeeze of lime juice, a lightly oaked Geelong chardonnay) and it came as a surprise to hear that whiting is one of the most-fished species around the eastern fringes of the Road.

How to prepare a globe artichoke

Winter is the best time to use artichokes. Choose large firm ones — tight without a ridge or bump on the globe. This is a good indication that the artichoke will not have formed the hairy choke. Leave the stalk attached. In a stainless steel pot put enough cold water to cover the artichokes and add the juice of some lemons. Cut the top quarter from the globes horizontally, peel away the tough outer leaves and pare the base of its fibrous outer layer. Peel down the stalk to reveal the tender white centre. Rub with lemon and cook in the acidulated water until cooked, about 15 minutes. Strain and dress with a good vinaigrette. When ready to serve cut lengthwise and dress with your favourite dressing.

The man who told me was Dennis White, a fish wholesaler of fifteen-years experience in St Leonards, near Queenscliff, so he should know. And I was surprised because I'd not seen local whiting promoted on too many local restaurant menus. But then Dennis enlightened me.

'I've sold whiting to local hotels and they've put it on the menu as South Australian,' he said, shaking his head. 'They just don't think.'

Which takes me back to the beginning of this chapter. You would have thought that the fishing and hotel industries, two of the oldest in the region, would have got their acts together after all this time. But in many ways, they are just as young and fragile as all the other food cultures here.

Organics in the Otways

Every Saturday morning during the season, the foreshore at Apollo Bay comes alive with its weekly market. Stalls selling crafts, paintings, clothes and aromatherapy kits are squeezed in among other stalls selling berries, spuds, pumpkins, lettuces — all produce of the many farms clustered in the Otways behind the town. (This market almost makes up for the fact that there is no good fruit and veg shop in Apollo Bay. There used to be, but it was bought out by the supermarket, where the young bloke at the checkout now has to ask you what the grassy-looking stuff in your trolley is, and you have to answer 'chives' without succumbing to the temptation to add 'ya dill'.)

If you take more than a passing glance at these fruit and veg stalls, you will notice that most of them are selling organic produce. Now I would have thought that the Otways were too cold and wet to grow vegies without resorting to pretty heavy duty fungicides and the like, but I realise I am very much mistaken. According to David Grimshaw, partner in the home-delivery company Living Organics, the western part of the Gellibrand Valley where he farms is suitable for growing almost anything — as are most of the sheltered folds of the Otways.

All right, so mangoes are out of the question. And attempting to grow dates might be considered a little foolish. But almost everything else is a goer.

'When I was doing a permaculture course a few years ago,' says Grimshaw, 'I knew of the Gellibrand Valley's reputation as a good place to grow things. When we got here we found that we could do well with all the cold weather fruit and veg — apples, berries, peas — but we also found we could grow Asian vegetables in hot houses.'

Berries are also a large part of Cornelius and Cornelia Bons' farm near Forrest. The almost impossibly named Dutch-born couple moved here fourteen years ago from the Dandenongs, where they had grown vegies organically for their six kids. They now grow a huge quantity of berries organically for the public — for the preserves and jams that Cornelia Bons makes and sells from the farm gate. But there are also vegies and herbs, and during the season, the Bons travel to Apollo Bay every Saturday.

Over the last few years, they have seen demand for their produce increase dramatically. 'We used to bring some things back home with us,' says Cornelia, 'but now we are usually completely sold out by midday.' David Grimshaw agrees: 'There is huge demand for organic produce, and it comes from right across the social spectrum, not just from the alternative lifestyle people in the area.'

Perhaps the time is right for somebody to open a fruit and veg shop again in Apollo Bay — and an organic one at that.

GENTLE ANNIE
"Pennyroyal Farm"
SILVANBERRY
PRESERVE
300g Net

A Picnic on the Barwon

Whole Foods Sourdough and Zen Artisan Ciabatta

Angel's Jamon with Fresh Figs

Portarlington Mussels with Red Pepper and Capers

Screaming Chicken

Small Leeks Braised in Pinot

Meredith Blue with Poppyseed Carackers

Raspberry Citrus Tart with Ricotta

Pick a spot, pack a basket. All the ingredients will be available in and around Geelong. Mr Deli in Malop Street is a fine Italian produce store and a good place to start.

Angel's Jamon with Fresh Figs

Cafe Botticelli, Geelong

The jamon is available at Mondo Deli in Pakington Street, Geelong West, or in Melbourne at Casa Iberica, Johnston Street, Fitzroy. They can also help with interstate suppliers.

Serves 10 as a picnic taste, 3 as an entree

10 slices of Angel Cardoso's jamon
2 tbsp extra virgin olive oil
1 tbsp balsamic vinegar
1 clove of garlic
salt and pepper
10 ripe figs, peeled and quartered
100 g rocket, well washed

Ask the deli to slice the jamon. Grill the jamon under an overhead grill until crisp, store in an airtight container.

Prepare a dressing with the oil, vinegar, garlic and seasonings. Pack the figs, rocket and jamon and assemble the salad at the last moment.

Portarlington Mussels with Red Pepper and Capers

Bazil's Foodstore, Geelong

The mussels cultivated in the bays around Geelong are small, sweet and flavoursome. They're a far cry from the large tough ones which were all we could obtain before mussel farming began in the district. Katos and Barwon Seafoods in Geelong sell local mussels and other good local seafood.

Serves 10 as a picnic treat, 3 as an entree

The Marinade

1 tbsp finely chopped white onion
1 tbsp finely chopped spring onions
3 tbsp chopped Italian parsley
1 tbsp finely chopped, de-seeded and peeled red pepper
1 tbsp finely chopped capers (choose the very small ones)
grated zest of one lemon
3 tbsp extra virgin olive oil
1 tbsp red wine vinegar (Minya Winery at Connewarre makes an excellent one)
salt and pepper
1 kg mussels

Mix all the marinade ingredients together. Clean any muddy residue from the mussel shells. Throw them into a large pan. Cover, cook for a few minutes, removing mussels as their shells open. Discard any whose shells do not open.

Remove mussel from shell, pull away beard, retain clean half of shell. Put mussels in a small bowl, with marinade, leave until the next day.

Serve mussels on the shell on their own, as part of the picnic food, or with a small salad as an entree.

menu 1: a picnic on the barwon

Screaming Chicken ✓

Screaming Seeds Spice Company, Bellbrae

This marinade is delicious for tofu, lamb, chicken, fish, seafood or beef. Mirin, a Japanese rice wine, can be bought from health food shops; as an alternative, use sweet or dry sherry instead. You can apply any Screaming Seeds spice blends to this marinade, as they all work just as brilliantly as the Kashmiri Krush. A fillet of lamb rolled and marinated in the above marinade for a couple of hours then panfried and sliced to serve warm over a salad is just as delicious. This marinade is excellent to use as a baste.

Serves 6

The Marinade

2 tsp Screaming Seeds Kashmiri Krush

1.5 kg fresh chicken

4 tsp olive oil

1 tsp finely chopped fresh herbs (optional)

6 tsp Mirin

2 tsp natural yoghurt (optional)

4 tsp soy sauce (if marinating tofu, omit the yoghurt)

Place above ingredients in a container that has a sealed lid. Rub marinade well into the chicken. Mix well and leave to marinate in the fridge for a minimum of 2 hours (overnight is better), mixing occasionally.

When ready, barbecue, roast or grill. Cool and pack into that essential 'Esky'.

Small Leeks Braised in Pinot ✗

Sunnybrae Country Restaurant, Birregurra

Clean 2 small leeks per person and slowly braise in pinot noir until tender (we use Spray Farm Pinot). The leeks will absorb the wine. When cool, moisten with a little olive oil and add a good pinch of black pepper.

Meredith Blue with Poppyseed Carackers

Meredith Blue is available at Vince and Rosa's Fruit and Veg, Pakingon Street, Geelong. Carackers from The Biscuit Tin, Drysdale.

Raspberry Citrus Tart with Ricotta ?

Pud's Pantry and Deli, Warrnambool

Serves 10

1 shortcrust pastry shell (25 cm)

4 free range eggs

100 g castor sugar

350 g fresh ricotta cheese

500 ml double cream

4 lemons, zested then juiced

100 g raspberries

clotted cream for garnish

Blind bake pastry case in a 180° C oven for approximately 10 minutes, or until the pastry has set and is beginning to develop a golden colour. Put the eggs, sugar, cheese, cream, lemon zest and juice into a food processor, then whiz until well combined.

Fill the pastry shell with lemon and cheese mixture then evenly place the raspberries on the top.

Bake at 150°C for 20-25 minutes. Allow to cool, then serve at room temperature with clotted cream.

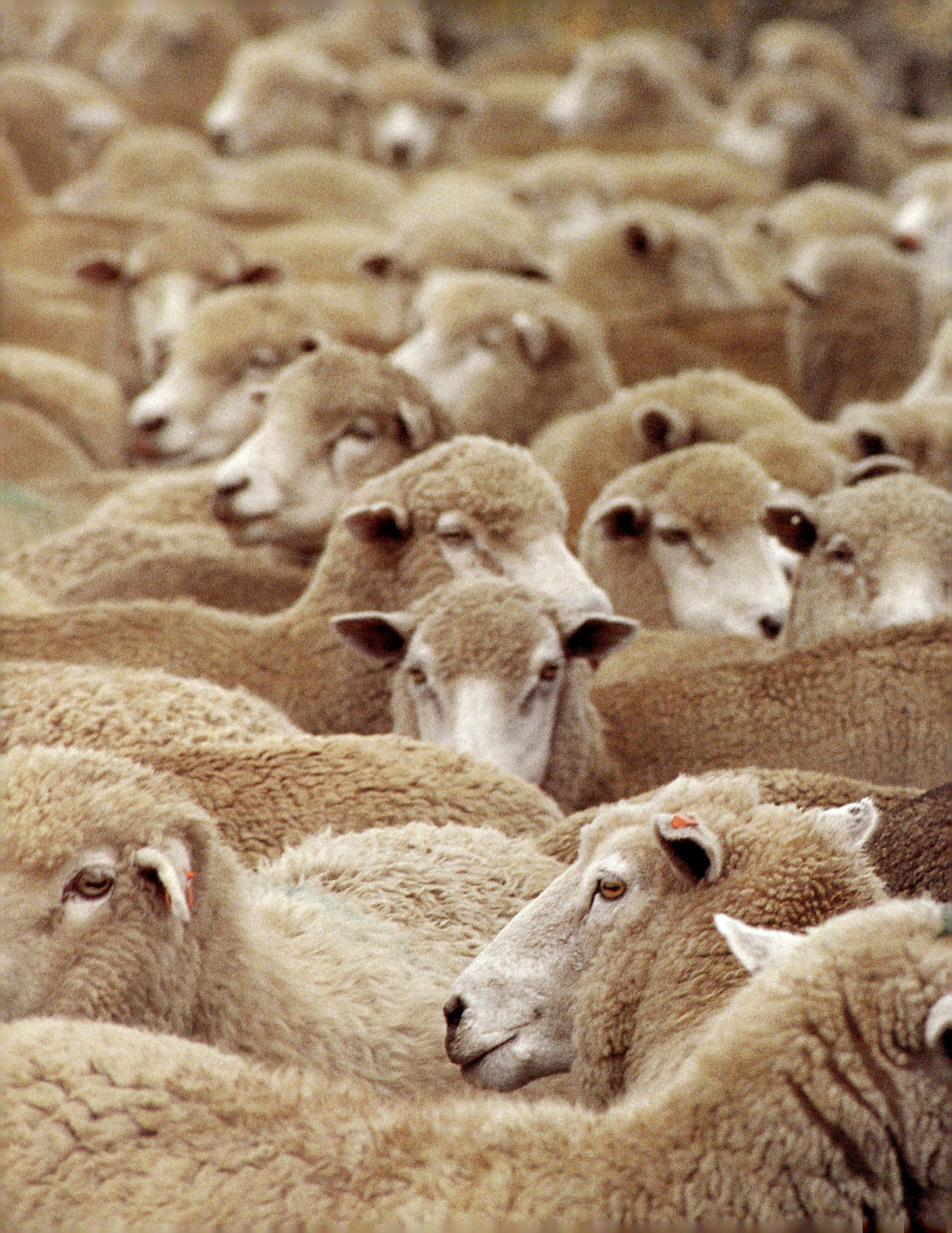

blessed are the cheesemakers

Picture this. The year is 1909. It's the height of summer. Mid-morning and already the sun is beginning to really burn through those few tall trees that have escaped the saw mills down here in the heart of the Otways. There you are, perched atop your shambly old cart, watching as the horse ahead of you negotiates the rough and ready track leading down to the dairy. It's dusty, dangerous and the last thing you want to do is lose your precious load of fresh milk.

Every bump and dint in the track makes the cool white liquid slosh ever-louder in the motley collection of dull grey tanks you've jammed onto the cart. You're glad indeed when you finally turn the last bend, quit the scant shade of ragged gums and head towards the welcome sight of the dairy. Red bricks. Cool shade. Perhaps a glass or two of beer.

Your family have been coming here ever since they settled in the area, thirty years ago. The butter and a little cheese that comes out the other end of the process has fed that family, given it rich, delicious sustenance.

Half a century later. A busy day at the big new dairy in town — as fine an example of modern industrial architecture as you could hope to find in the western districts. Shining tankers, spanking new vans emblazoned with the company logo, truck cheese and butter out, destined for the supper tables of people in Geelong, Melbourne and as far afield as London.

Inside, encased in their pristine interior, technicians fiddle with bright dials, white-coated workers supervise the cheesemaking machinery, the smell of cleanliness is everywhere. Dairying in this part of the world has grown from a cottage industry to a huge industry. Allansford, home of the Warrnambool Butter and Cheese Factory is affectionately known as cheese town.

And flash forward again, this time to the end of the twentieth century. The big industry is still there: Kraft is the name you'll see emblazoned on the tankers and trucks swarming around the dairies now. There are plenty of people benefiting from the dairy industry, too: Regal Ice Cream in Colac springs rather sweetly to mind. A double scoop of Regal's best flavour — blueberry cheesecake — on a warm summer's evening in Apollo Bay or Lorne, is about the tastiest way to experience this benefit.

But the cottage dairy industry has returned with a vengeance, too, motivated amongst other things by the desire to make great cheese. Well, okay, describing this motley crew of renaissance cheesemakers as an 'industry' might be pushing it a bit (you can count on one hand the number of them holding the banner aloft in the region) but what it lacks in size, this small group more than makes up for in quality and enthusiasm.

Timboon

Hermann Schulz was the pioneer. When he started making small-scale, hand-crafted cheese on his farm at Timboon, just inland from Port Campbell, he had nobody to swap ideas or experiences with in that part of the world. As we shall see, he had also decided to adopt an unconventional approach to raising his cattle for milking, so the move was in some ways doubly brave.

Schulz and his wife Marlis bought their 96-hectare farm at Timboon in the early 1970s. Schulz had been working in the building trade around Australia since arriving from Germany some years before, but decided it was time to put his agricultural education to good use. He decided to run cattle and, inspired by the popularity of the movement in Germany at the time, he also decided from the start to run the farm along Biodynamic principles.

Right • Hermann Schulz.

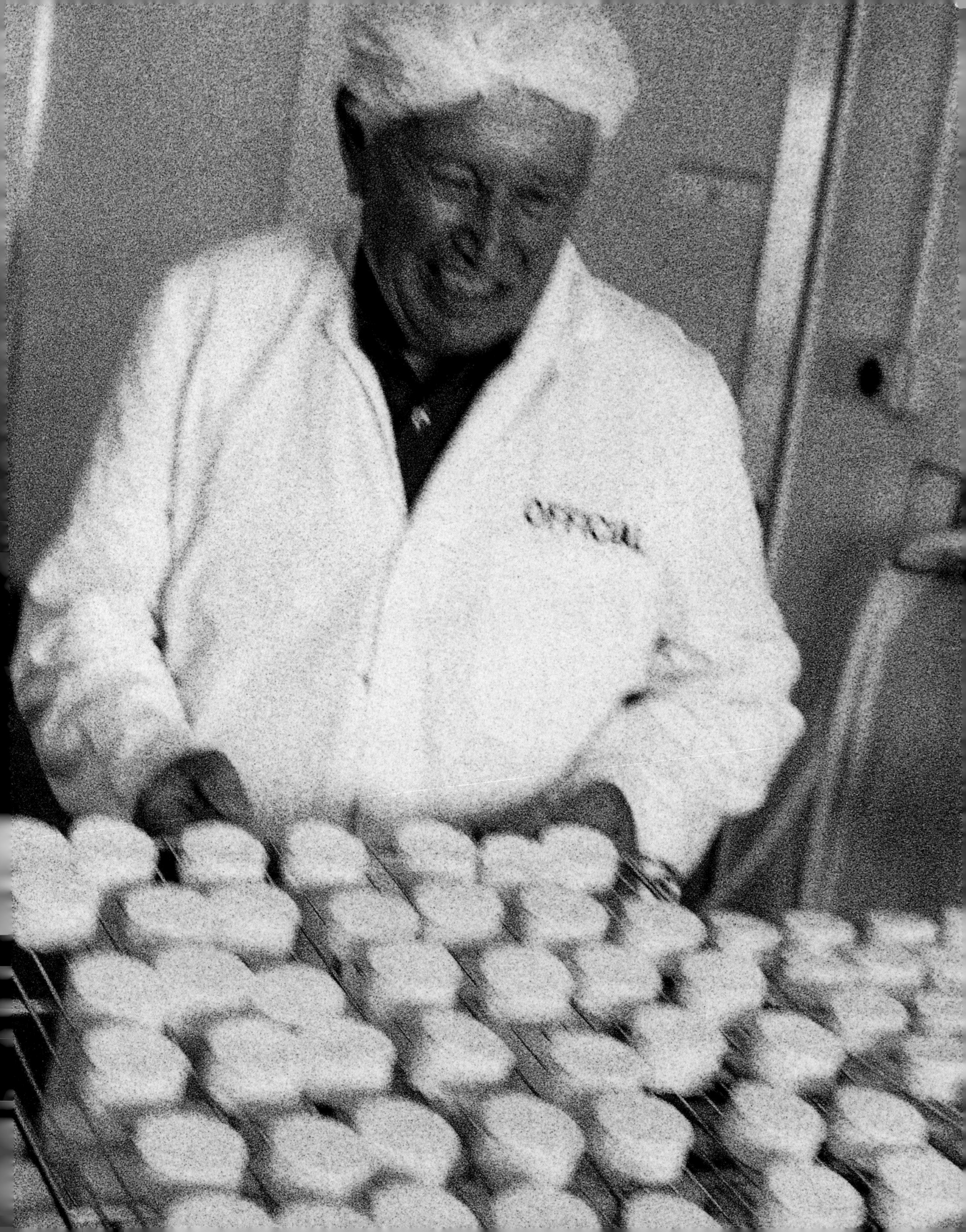
OFFICIAL

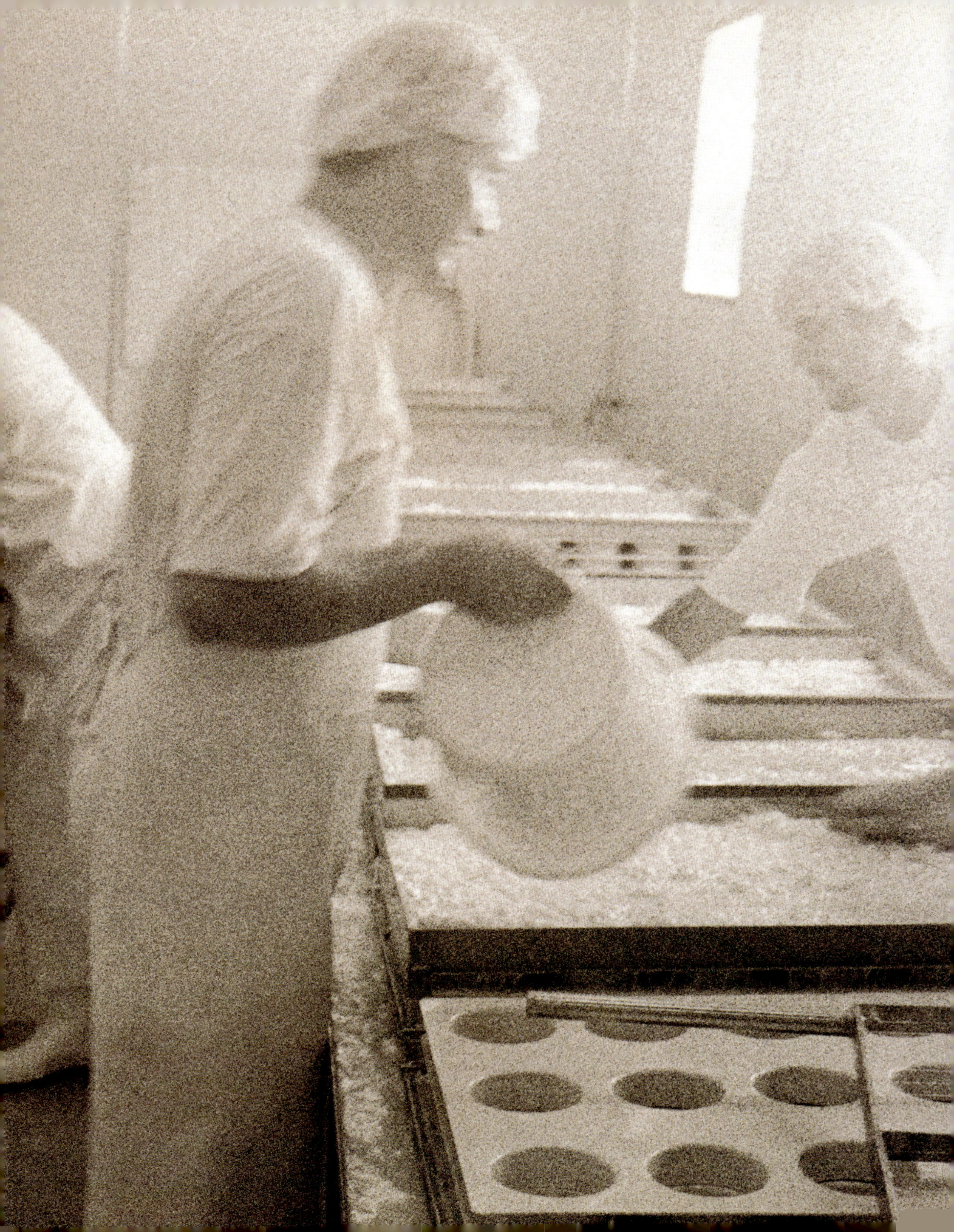

Biodynamics, as you may be aware, can be described as turbo-charged organic agriculture. So as well as the avoidance of artificial fertilisers and herbicides, there is also an active program of adding revitalising or dynamising natural preparations to the soil to increase its vitality. Today, many farms across Australia are switching back to organic practice, with a few delving into the nether reaches of Biodynamics — but a quarter of a century ago it was pretty unusual stuff.

Not surprisingly (depending on your point of view), the farm responded well. More importantly, the cows that grazed on the grass that grew on the farm responded even better.

'We started selling our milk to the big dairies,' says Hermann. 'But we soon found that the milk coming from our cows was of a special quality, and when the Kraft tankers came in it just got lost. So eventually we decided to keep some back and use it ourselves.'

This was 1984. Things started small — a few little camemberts here, some slightly larger bries there — but swiftly grew as word got out that there was more to life in Timboon that processed cheese slices. The business slowly grew, and cheese-lovers further afield — in Melbourne, further even — began to beat a slow trail to the Schulz's door.

Today, Timboon is a huge success story. The Schulz family recently sold the business to the King Island Company, though Hermann remains as a consultant, and daughter Audrey is managing director. Son Michael share-farms a neighbouring property to provide Timboon with more milk.

A beautifully neat, cottage-style garden at the property welcomes tens of thousands of visitors each year to the tasting room and shop. The Timboon range of cheeses,

Pictured • Timboon cheesemakers.

from spreadable brie in a jar (surprisingly good) to the intense and tangy blues Timboonzola and St Joseph, is available for tasting. Some local wines are also offered, as are other foods — including Screaming Seeds spice mixes and, rather odd but tempting, QA mettwurst from the not-so-local Barossa Valley.

White mould cheeses, the bries and camemberts (or Berties as he likes to call them) that Hermann started with are still the biggest part of Timboon's production. And incredibly reliable they are, too. You are safe buying Timboon cheese. But then they have to be reliable: the cheeses sell in supermarkets across the country, and Hermann does a steady trade in portion-packed Berties for airlines.

Unlike some other boutique or farmhouse cheesemakers, such broad commercialism doesn't sit uneasily with Hermann Schulz. 'I like to make cheese today and sell it tomorrow,' he says, bluntly. It's one of the reasons he has never produced time-consuming, hard cheeses like cheddar styles. It's also one of the reasons why his cheeses are so reliable.

But in some ways, because of this attitude (and because of intransigent food laws that forbid the manufacture or import of unpasteurised cheese in this country), we are prevented from tasting the very best cheese that could be produced at Timboon.

A few years ago, before those laws became set in stone, I had the opportunity to taste a camembert Hermann made with unpasteurised milk. And I can still taste it now: incredibly complex, deeply creamy and developed, long-tasting and more than slightly wild — full with the flavour of the biodynamic milk. Delicious, yes, reliable, no. Perhaps the fact that it was unpasteurised was incidental. Perhaps it was just a particularly good batch of cheese. The point is, we'll never know.

Mount Emu Creek

You know a family has some clout in a region when main streets of major towns carry that family's name. In the case of the vast sweeping western districts of Victoria around Camperdown, the name you'll see in the main street is Manifold. In the second half of the nineteenth century, the Manifolds owned most of this country — just on 270 square km — at one point. Their descendants are still regarded by some as the closest thing the district has to landed gentry.

The three Manifold brothers arrived from England in 1838, and set out into the extraordinary unknown west of Melbourne determined to find their fortune. They got as far as Lake Purrumbete, just to the east of Camperdown, and stopped, deciding — reasonably enough — that this is where their destiny lay (the story of this journey, in the form of letters sent home, was later published as *The Wished-For Land*).

Before long, a large, sprawling residence had been built on the shores of the lake, and the Purrumbete station became quite the social venue for passing artists and socialites — Eugène von Guérard was one among many who painted this wide open country. At the turn of the century, the thoroughly Victorian mansion that had evolved at Purrumbete was renovated in a thoroughly art nouveau fashion, with designs by Robert Purchas, murals by Walter Withers, a founder of the Heidelberg school, and intricate organic wood carving by Robert Prenzel. It was — and is — one of Australia's most stunning homesteads ... but more of Purrumbete later.

In 1877, William Manifold decided to begin dairying at Purrumbete, and soon built the operation up to be one of the biggest in the Western District, with the company's Pelikan brand butter exported in huge quantity to the

UK. By the First World War, however, the dairy had closed and the Manifold family had begun spreading, occupying two other homes in the district as well as the rambling Purrumbete.

Flash forward to 1999. It's a dusty, glary day just outside Camperdown. Hundreds of beige sheep have been herded into holding pens, waiting to be milked. Gates clang. A tall bloke shouts obscenities at the sheep dogs, darting and jumping over and through the seething flock.

I'm standing under a water tank trying to get some respite from the glare, talking to another bloke wearing a floppy hat, a permanent sardonic grin and weatherbeaten Hard Yakka blues. This is Robert Manifold, and, like his ancestor over a century ago, he has decided to get into dairying.

In 1993 Manifold, like many other graziers in Victoria, was becoming increasingly fed-up with the depressed state of the wool market. So he and a few others decided to have a go at milking sheep as a way of value-adding their product. In the first year they simply wanted to find out whether it was possible and it quickly became clear that it was.

The next year, Manifold began to wonder whether he couldn't value-add a little further by turning that milk into yoghurt. But yoghurt involved full-time manufacture and a factory. The other farmers weren't keen, so Manifold and his wife, Louise, bought them out.

'We soon found that yoghurt is a fiercely competitive market,' says Manifold, grinning. 'And there had been little-to-no marketing of

Above • Robert Manifold and Western Districts dog.

sheep's milk yoghurt up that point. So we decided to make cheese. Now the cheese has taken over.'

They leased a corner of the Bonlac cheese factory in Camperdown, decided to take the name of a local landmark as their brand, and hired a cheesemaker, John Staaks — a man who was immediately sensitive to the Manifolds' needs. 'The dairy industry in Australia is enormous,' says Manifold. 'It involves thousands of cheesemakers. But — and it's a huge but — there's a chasm between push-button cheesemaking and hand-making cheese. Specialist cheese relies on our senses — you are hands-on working with the curd.'

The yoghurt is still made and is very good indeed: pure white touched with hints of green — fresh, lively, grassy. But the cheeses are lovely. Fresh ricotta is very fine, not too creamy, clean; Romney Fresca is a semi-hard cheese with good sweet, nutty flavour; Mount Elephant is a tangy, crumbly pecorino-style with good length of flavour. Another cheese is also made from time to time, a cloth-bound Romney that is aged for a year or more. Due to the inexact science of such ageing — and the relative inexperience of the makers — these wild-looking, dark-coloured cheeses are either sensational (like the most extraordinarily complex aged pecorino) or disgustingly infected. More consistency will come with more experience — but at least they're having a go.

Mount Emu Creek cheeses and yoghurt have been a big success in delis and restaurants across Australia — especially Sydney where, according to Manifold, people are a bit more adventurous in their pursuit of new tastes. In his local market, though, people are far more concerned about price — a specialist cheese is

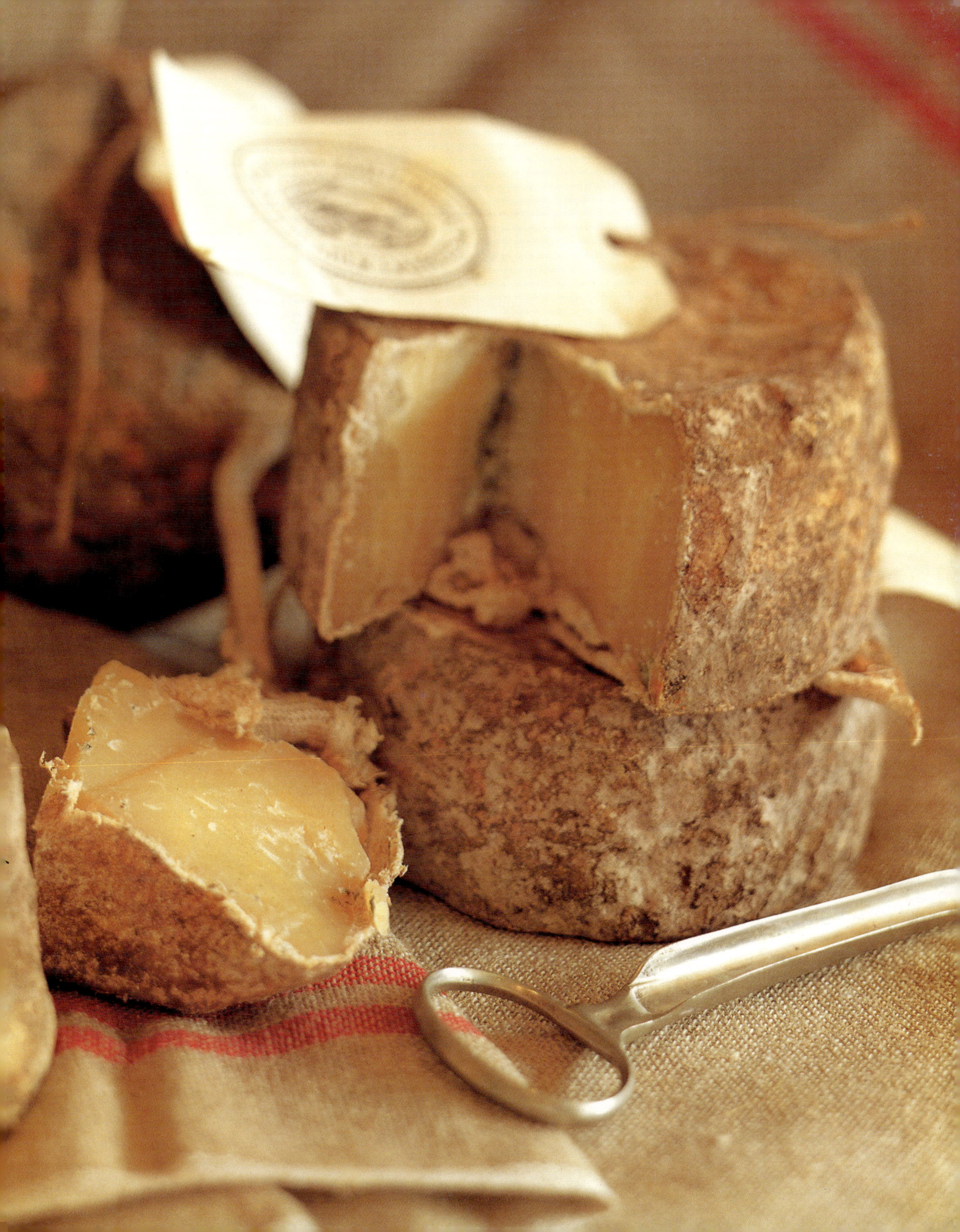

perceived as being far too expensive, regardless of its proximity of production.

Following in the previous Manifolds' footsteps again, Mount Emu Creek has also cracked the export market — almost. 'Three consignments of cheese went to Hong Kong a couple of years ago,' says Manifold. 'It was all going well and then everything came to a grinding halt around the same time as the Chinese takeover and One Nation appearing. But there's tremendous potential there, provided we maintain quality and supply.'

Manifold is perhaps more acutely aware than some of his place in history. A little while later, standing in Manifold's living room, I look through the picture window at an incredible panorama of grazing land and hills stretching to the distance.

'Master of all you survey,' I say, half-joking.

'Once,' says Manifold, more than half-serious. Then we sit at the big table and talk about how unusual such Mediterranean styles of cheese as ricotta and pecorino must seem in a culture so steeped in Anglo-Saxon food heritage (Yorkshire pudding and roast beef in the middle of summer is the Western District's way). He brings out dusty old volumes charting the history of dairying in Victoria — pictures of busty young dairy maids and lusty young dairy lads. He talks about how Australia is changing forever, from a country that really did ride on the sheep's back to one that is becoming so urbanised.

And then he gets up to make another espresso in his sleek stainless-steel espresso machine.

Shaw River

Buffalo are the most mesmerising creatures. Huddled together under a big old tree on a threatening grey afternoon, the slow beasts with their gracefully chunky horns seem to suck light into their thick slate-purple hides. Covered in caked mud from wallowing, breathing clouds of moist air through their big soft nostrils, they seem to cause time itself to slow down around them.

But these buffalo aren't lounging around under a tree in western Victoria just for writers to waffle about and photographers to shoot (although it's almost reason enough). Oh no. These animals are here to work.

Roger and Sue Haldane imported these great dark beasts seven years ago. At the time it was revolutionary (it still is), as nobody had thought much beyond the conventional cow, sheep and goat sources of milk for cheesemaking (they still aren't). But then Roger Haldane is far from a conventional farmer.

For a start, the Haldanes are the former owners of the big, rambling Purrumbete homestead, with its art nouveau murals and carvings — far from a conventional place to live. (Since the first edition of this book, they have sold Purrembete and bought a farm at Shaw River, near Yambuk.) When the Haldanes bought Purrumbete and the surrounding 168 hectares of land over eight years ago to run as a farm, it hadn't been part of the Manifold family for ages (other owners in its recent tempestuous past include David Marriner and Rene Rivkin).

From the beginning though, it was to be no ordinary farm. Haldane had already been one of the pioneers of the breeding of alpacas in Australia; he still has some, including a particularly cute and possessive brown one that thinks it's the family dog. And before that he had worked as an illustrator — winning awards

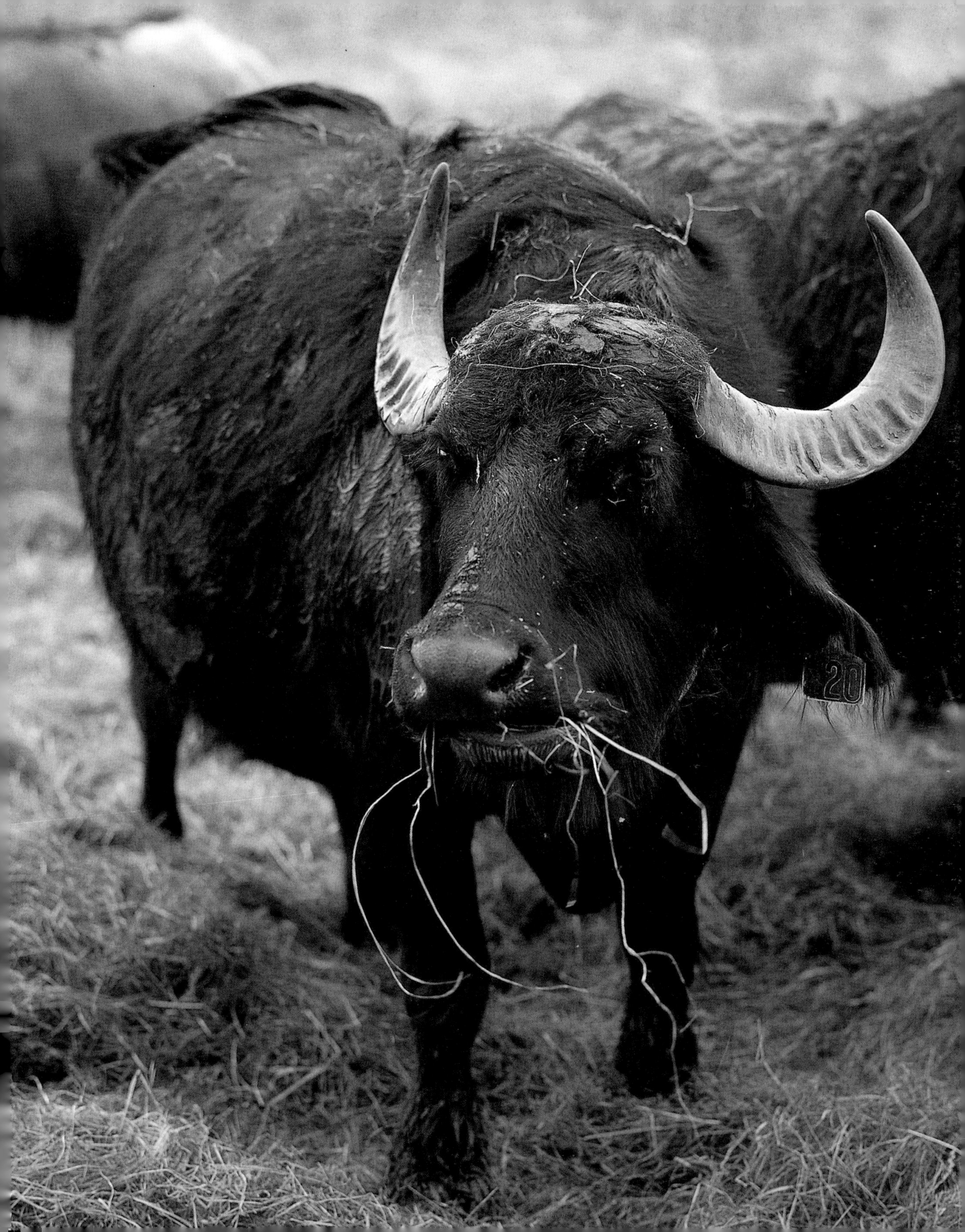
20

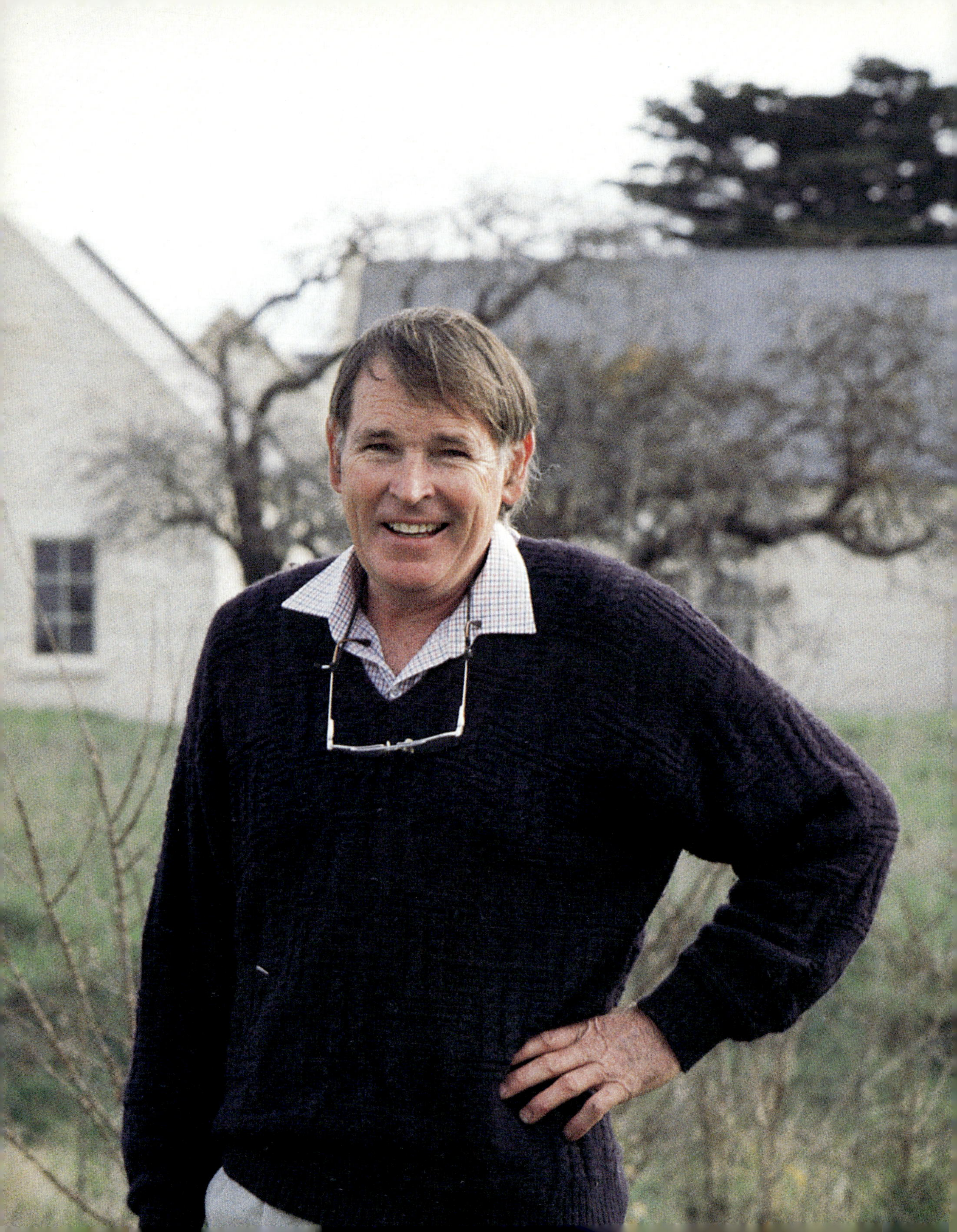

for work on books with Colin Thiele (Haldane's designs grace the Shaw River labels). He also plays the bagpipes. You get the picture.

Deciding to be the first people in Australia to make real buffalo yoghurt and mozzarella, then, seemed like a perfectly natural thing to do. Getting the animals from near Naples, in Italy, was the relatively easy part. Making the cheese has proved harder — and selling it harder still.

Haldane did his research, including a trip to Italy with Nick Haddow from the Richmond Hill Cafe and Larder cheese room in Melbourne. He found that although Italy is the world's centre for buffalo milk production, other places such as Bulgaria, Yugoslavia, South America and Greece all have histories of milking the big, slow animals.

This research, and continued experimentation at the Mount Emu Creek-leased part of the Bonlac dairy in nearby Camperdown has meant ever-increasing quality. The yoghurt and cheese were good when they were first launched, but they are much, much better now.

The yoghurt is arguably Australia's best, with an almost impossible whiteness of colour — very nearly blue, it's so startlingly reflective — and a thrilling intensity of fresh, clean, tangy, light-milky flavour. Sweet without sugar, finely textured and complex. I love it (in case you hadn't noticed). I'm not the only one: it is an exceptional yoghurt to put into other dishes, either savoury (the best tzatziki or raita you'll ever have) or sweet (either with a touch of blue gum honey swirled through, or served simply with berries).

The mozzarella (or bocconcini, depending how pedantic you're feeling) is very nearly in the same class (some would say it's better):

Left • Roger Haldane at his new Shaw River property.

SHAW RIVER
PRODUCT OF AUSTRALIA
DANCING BROLGA
THE ORIGINAL AUSTRALIAN BUFFALO CHEESE

wonderfully deep and milky in flavour, with an underlying sweet animal character and, again, excellent texture — just fibrous and stretchy enough, but soft, giving at the same time.

Roger Haldane loves his buffalo. So would you if they gave you the kind of milk they give him. He has names for them all. He only wishes that more people would feel the same way. 'In Italy, mozzarella is part of the culture, like bread or potatoes, and people are prepared to pay for good mozzarella,' he says. 'Here, too many people just think it's too expensive. People in this area, for example, should be excited about their local product. They should support it, like they support their local footy team. It will happen, over time. It's just a matter of building that culture.'

Fed up with waiting for Mohammed to come to the mountain though, the Haldanes have decided to take the mountain to Mohammed. At the time of writing, they are nearing completion of a dairy and sales outlet at Yambuk, near Port Fairy. It seems like a long way from Camperdown, but there are two good reasons for going there: the excellent passing trade for one, and the fact that Roger Haldane was born in Port Fairy, the grandson of the lighthouse-keeper.

So now Purrembete Buffalo Cheese is Shaw River Buffalo Cheese, and Roger's herd of buffalo wallows in the mud and lounges under the trees of its new home near Yambuk.

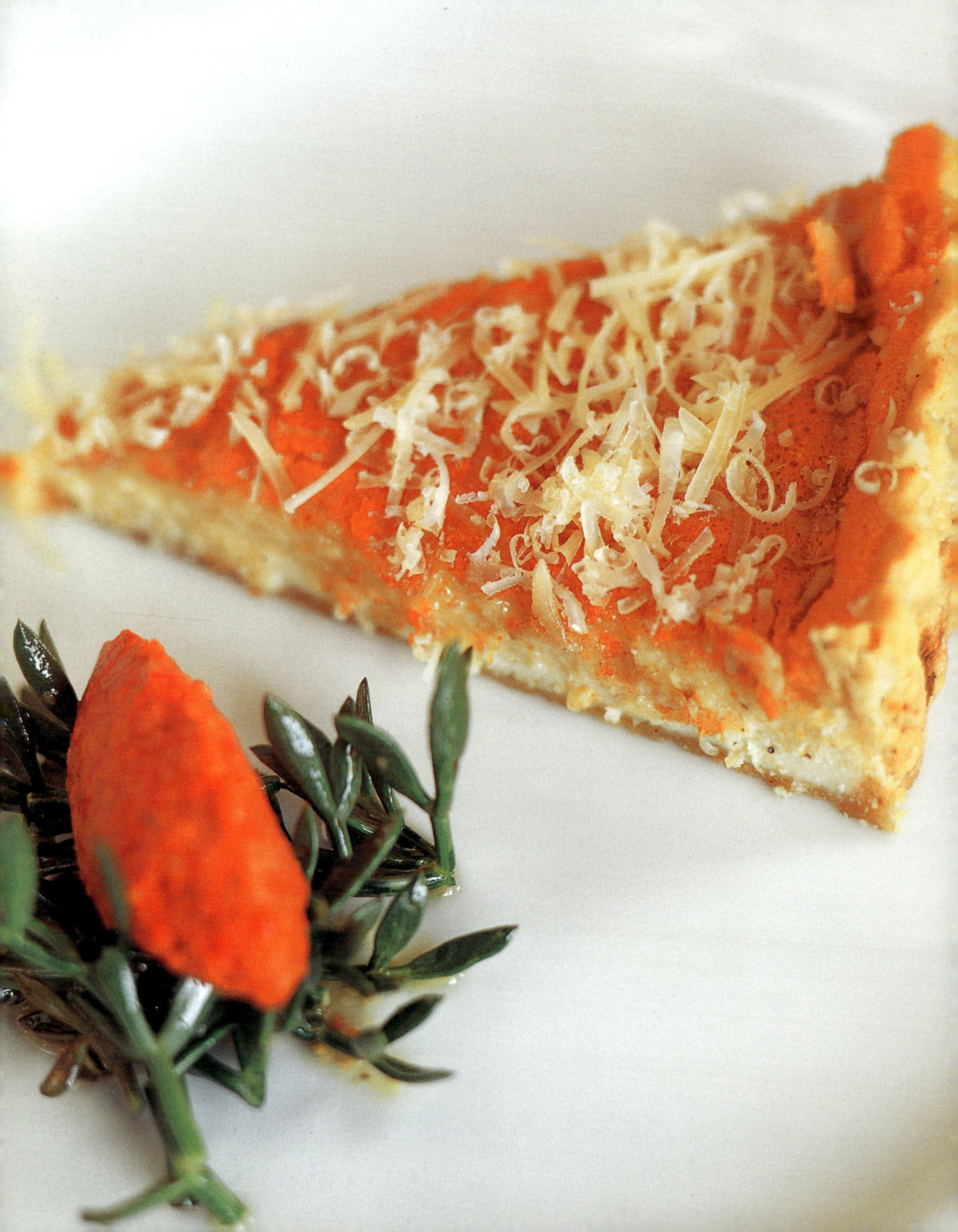

A Family Celebration

Chris's Kakavia - Greek Seafood Soup

Mt Elephant Pecorino Tart with Provencale Paste

Fricassee of Meredith Milk-fed Lamb

Cous Cous Fruit Cake
with Orange Blossom Water and Pistachio

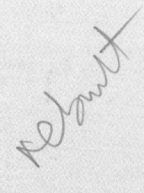

Chris's Kakavia — Greek Seafood Soup

Chris's Beacon Point Restaurant, Skenes Creek

Serves 8

1 large onion
1 large carrot
4 large potatoes
4 sticks celery
2 cloves garlic
½ cup olive oil
1 litre good fish stock

800 g selection of fresh fish (for example, 300 g fresh fillets of hapuka, 12 mussels, 12 large prawns, 200 g calamari, crayfish or crab legs)

salt and pepper

1 cup cream

Peel and chop vegetables into 2-3 cm pieces. Gently saute onion and garlic in a large saucepan. When soft, not coloured, add remaining vegetables. Cover with a well-sealed lid and braise the vegetables until very soft.

Puree cooked vegetables until smooth, adding a small amount of the stock if necessary.

Return vegetable puree to the saucepan and blend in remaining stock until a smooth consistency is reached. Gently bring to simmering. Add fish and seafood and poach until just cooked.

Season and add cream, and keep warm until serving. Do not bring to the boil.

Mt Elephant Pecorino Tart with Provençale Paste

Sunnybrae Country Restaurant, Birregurra

Serves 10

For 500 g Short Pastry

200 g unsalted butter
250 g flour
1 large egg
1 tsp porcini powder
1 tbsp milk
pinch of salt

Cut the butter into small pieces and rub into the flour with the egg and porcini powder. Add the milk and salt — do not overwork. Wrap in plastic wrap and leave to rest.

Roll out between 2 sheets of 'Go-Between' to a little larger than your flan (remember the depth).

Blind bake the tart shell.

Provençale Paste

100 g roasted capsicum
100 g blanched almonds
20 g anchovies
30 g raisins
5 ml orange blossom water
2 cloves garlic
pinch of ground fennel seeds
1 tsp balsamic vinegar
1 tsp truffle oil

Blend all ingredients in a food processor to a smooth paste.

Filling for 28 cm tart case

9 large eggs
300 g Mt Elephant pecorino
300 g cream (35% fat), lightly whipped
salt and pepper
50 g Parmesan for top

Mix together all the ingredients, except Parmesan, for the filling. Fill the tart shell and bake at 125°C for 45 minutes.

Serve at room temperature sprinkled with Parmesan, accompanied by some of the Provencal paste.

Fricassee of Meredith Milk-fed Lamb

Kostas, Lorne

Serves 6

- 1 kg baby milk-fed lamb, pieces approx 100g each (if possible, include offal, liver, kidney, heart)
- flour
- ½ cup olive oil
- 1 cup dry white wine
- 2 green cos lettuce hearts, washed and sliced into 1 cm ribbons
- 2 bunches spring onions, chopped
- 1 head of green spring garlic, chopped
- 1 bunch of dill, chopped

Season pieces of meat and lightly dust with flour. Heat the olive oil in the bottom of a large saucepan. Fry the meat lightly, two or three pieces at a time until brown and remove into a side dish.

When all the meat is sealed but still rare, place it all back into the pan with any juices that have run out. Pour in the cup of dry white wine to deglaze the pan, and boil rapidly for a minute. Add the shredded cos lettuce, the spring onions, spring garlic and the chopped dill. Return the pan to heat with a tight fitting lid and cook on moderate heat for about 10-15 minutes.

Serve in deep plates with the juices poured around the meat and greens, with some crusty white bread.

Cous Cous Fruit Cake with Orange Blossom Water and Pistachio

Wholefoods Cafe, Geelong

Serves 10

- 1 cup orange juice
- 1 tbsp Cointreau
- 1 tsp orange blossom water
- grated rind of one orange
- 250 g white palm sugar
- 120 g dried figs, each de-stemmed, and cut into 4
- 100 g raisins
- 150 g dried apricots, each cut into 4
- 1 cinnamon stick
- 200 ml water
- 1 ½ cups dried cous cous
- 2 tbsp chopped pistachio nuts
- carob flour
- pomegranate molasses (available at good Italian delis)

The Syrup • Combine the orange juice, Cointreau, blossom water, rind and the palm sugar in a small saucepan and simmer to combine the flavours, and reduce. Set aside.

The Cake • To begin, reconstitute the dried fruit by simmering with some water and the cinnamon stick until the fruit is swollen and plumped. Remove the stick and set aside.

Combine 100 ml of the syrup with 200 ml of water, place in a saucepan and bring to the boil. Remove from the heat and stir in the cous cous to swell and take up the liquid. Allow to sit for a few minutes.

Now mix the fruit and the cous cous together, thoroughly. The resultant mixture can now be turned into an oiled 24 cm-springform pan, pressed down and levelled off. Place the cake in the fridge, to cool, for 30 minutes. Invert onto a platter and dress with some of the syrup, scatter the surface with pistachio nuts, dust with carob flour and serve with a drizzle of pomegranate molasses.

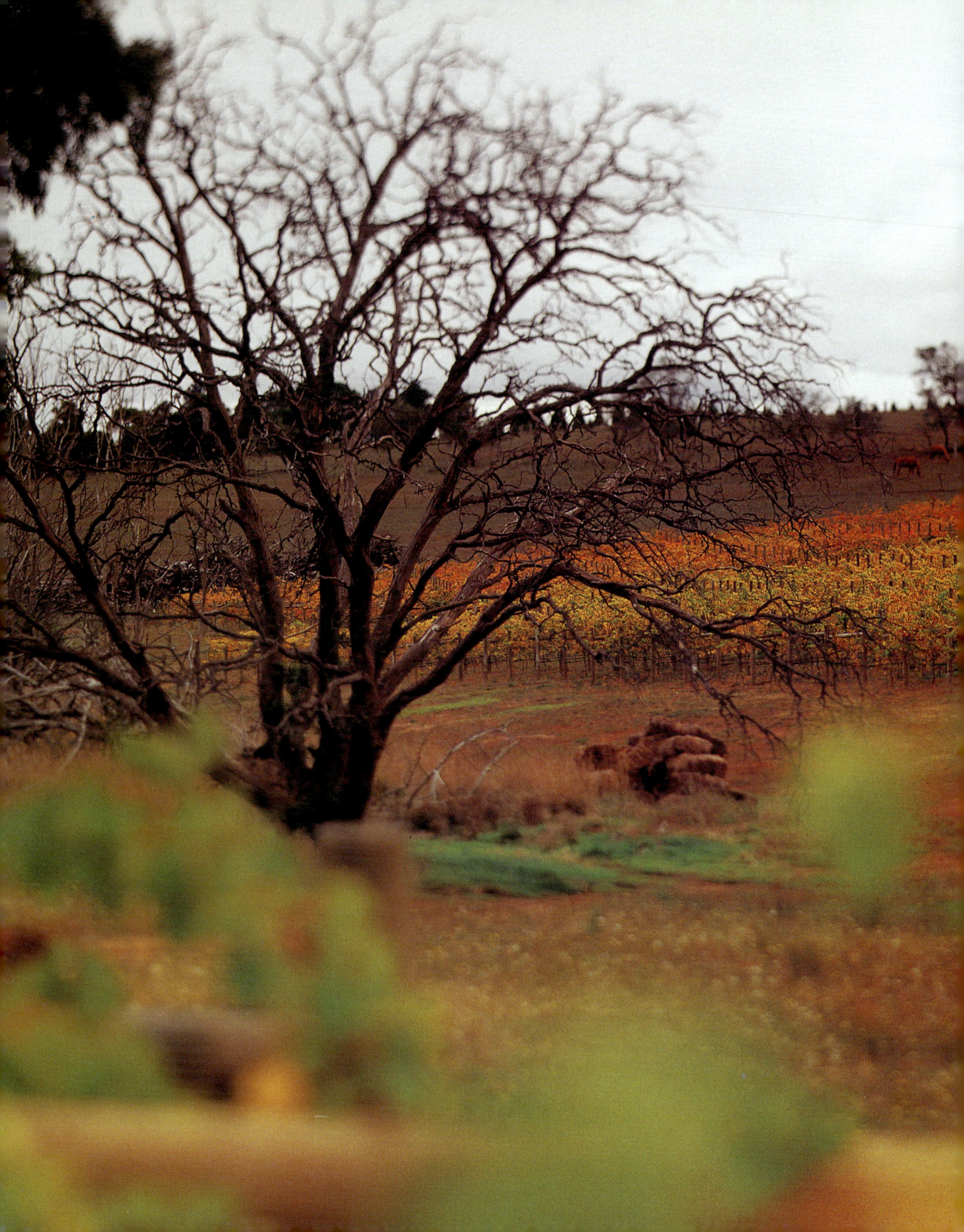

the grape treaders
vineyards • wines • winemakers

It all started so well. One hundred and forty years ago, the land around Geelong was covered in vines. Well, okay, not quite covered: there were a few parts of the rolling countryside to the north, west and south of the burgeoning township that weren't thriving vineyards. There were a couple of farms as well.

No, seriously, in the 1850s and 1860s Geelong was the most important wine region in Victoria — more important even in terms of acreage than the now more famous Yarra Valley, to the east of Melbourne. Swiss and German settlers, enticed to the colony by its first governor, Charles La Trobe, had established hundreds of small vineyards — and a few larger ones — in the Moorabool Valley, along the gentle slopes of the Barrabool Hills, at Waurn Ponds, and at Germantown, now known as Grovedale.

In 1865, the Geelong region accounted for almost a quarter of Victoria's 1600 hectares of vines. And interestingly, the grape varieties that were among the most widely planted and considered the best quality included hermitage (which we know today as shiraz) and Burgundy (pinot noir).

The thoroughly European names of Belperroud, Pettavel and Dardel were well known then. These men owned impressive, well-tended vineyards, and their wines — in a light, European style — were highly prized in Geelong, in Melbourne and Europe. Geelong, with its busy seaport, became quite a hub of wine trade activity, both exporting and importing. Melburnians and the new gold-rich at this time had an almost insatiable thirst for champagne.

So, it started well. What happened? Well, it ended suddenly and very traumatically, that's what happened. In the 1870s, barely two-decades old, the Geelong wine industry was the first in Australia to be attacked by the dramatically named vine louse, phylloxera vastatrix. The louse infests the vine's roots, slowly strangling it, and was in the process of devastating the vineyards of Europe. It had probably arrived in Geelong on vine cuttings, which were freely imported from Europe at the time, until legislation stopped the practice.

The government of the day responded viciously in an attempt to stem the tide of the pest, ordering the eradication of Geelong's vineyards. Within ten years all but a couple of out-of-the-way plots of vines had been destroyed (and these small, straggly vineyards were to disappear through neglect and disinterest before long).

Nothing much happened then. Not just in Geelong, but across the state: for the first two-thirds of the twentieth century, Victoria as a whole saw very little wine activity, apart from in the north-east around Rutherglen, and at isolated spots such as Tahbilk and Great Western.

But the 1960s saw the birth of the boutique winery movement across Australia, and vineyards sprang up once more in Geelong — increasing in number once cool-climate viticulture became popular. (While not as cool or wet as Mornington on the other side of Port Phillip Bay, Geelong is still far from warm.)

In 1966, Daryl Sefton, great-grandson of one of the original Swiss settlers, and his wife Nini established Idyll Vineyard in the Moorabool Valley, north-west of Geelong. A better couple could not have been chosen to reinvigorate the region: the wines have always been generous, warm in style; Nini's labels are colourful, bold; export has, from the beginning, played a huge role — particularly to Germany; and the pair are tireless and vocal promoters of Geelong.

The Seftons were joined in 1968 by Geelong identity, Tom Maltby, who planted a stunningly sited vineyard on the lower slopes of Mount Anakie, north of Geelong. The vineyard was subsequently run by the Hickinbotham family (now located on the Mornington Peninsula) who made some wonderful wines, particularly from cabernet sauvignon; it is now run by Otto Zambelli. Ken and Joy Campbell followed in 1970 with the small and underrated Mount Duneed Vineyard and Winery just off the arrow-straight Torquay road.

In 1973, Geelong businessman Stuart Hooper planted the district's best-known vineyard at Bannockburn, north-west of the city and, in 1975, Bruce Hyett replanted some pinot noir on one small part of the old Prince Albert vineyard site at Waurn Ponds established by David Pettavel over a century before.

The 1980s saw a few more vineyards pop up in the Geelong district, as the cool-climate fever intensified and some of the better Geelong pinot noirs and chardonnays began to filter onto the market: Austin's Barrabool and Waybourne Winery in Waurn Ponds; Staughton Vale, just around the hill from Mount Anakie; and Innisfail at Batesford; as well as Bannockburn winemaker Gary Farr with his own vineyard at Clyde Park. The vine began to creep into the wide, windswept country of the Bellarine Peninsula during this time, too: first the large Scotchmans Hill Vineyard, then the much smaller Kilgour Estate.

The 1990s have seen mostly consolidation and expansion. Scotchmans bought the impressive Spray Farm property and planted vines; Clyde Park was sold at least twice; Kilgour put in a restaurant; lots of people planted to sell their grapes. But no new wineries went up — with a kind of exception.

The Melbourne Wine Company was originally established by Melbourne restaurateur and entrepreneur Donlevy Fitzpatrick, the intention being to source fruit from the Greater Melbourne region and produce wines for everyday consumption, innovatively packaged in champagne bottles with crown seals (to counter the effects of cork taint).

When Fitzpatrick bought Clyde Park in the mid-1990s, the MWC winemaking operations moved there from their base on the Mornington Peninsula. He subsequently sold the vineyard, but winemakers Scott Ireland and Martin Williams inherited the label. They are still based in the Geelong region, and while the majority of grapes are sourced locally — particularly pinot noir, chardonnay and pinot gris — they continue to blend wines from other Melbourne regions.

Only a couple of other vineyards have been established outside the Geelong and Bellarine regions that are still operating and that could be considered local to the Great Ocean Road (other than those of the far south-west of the state, which are dealt with later in this chapter). One of these is a small vineyard near Colac originally called Barongavale, now owned and run by Melbourne wine broker, Rohan Little and producing good wines under the Red Rock and Otways Wines labels. The other is a new winery joint venture involving Langtons Wine Auctions at Werribee Mansion called Dark Horse. Winemaker Matt Harrop makes his first wines there this year: at the time of writing they are probably still fermenting. It will be a development to watch.

Despite all this activity, the Geelong region as a whole doesn't have the reputation for quality winemaking that its neighbours in the 'Melbourne Dress Circle' (the Yarra, Macedon

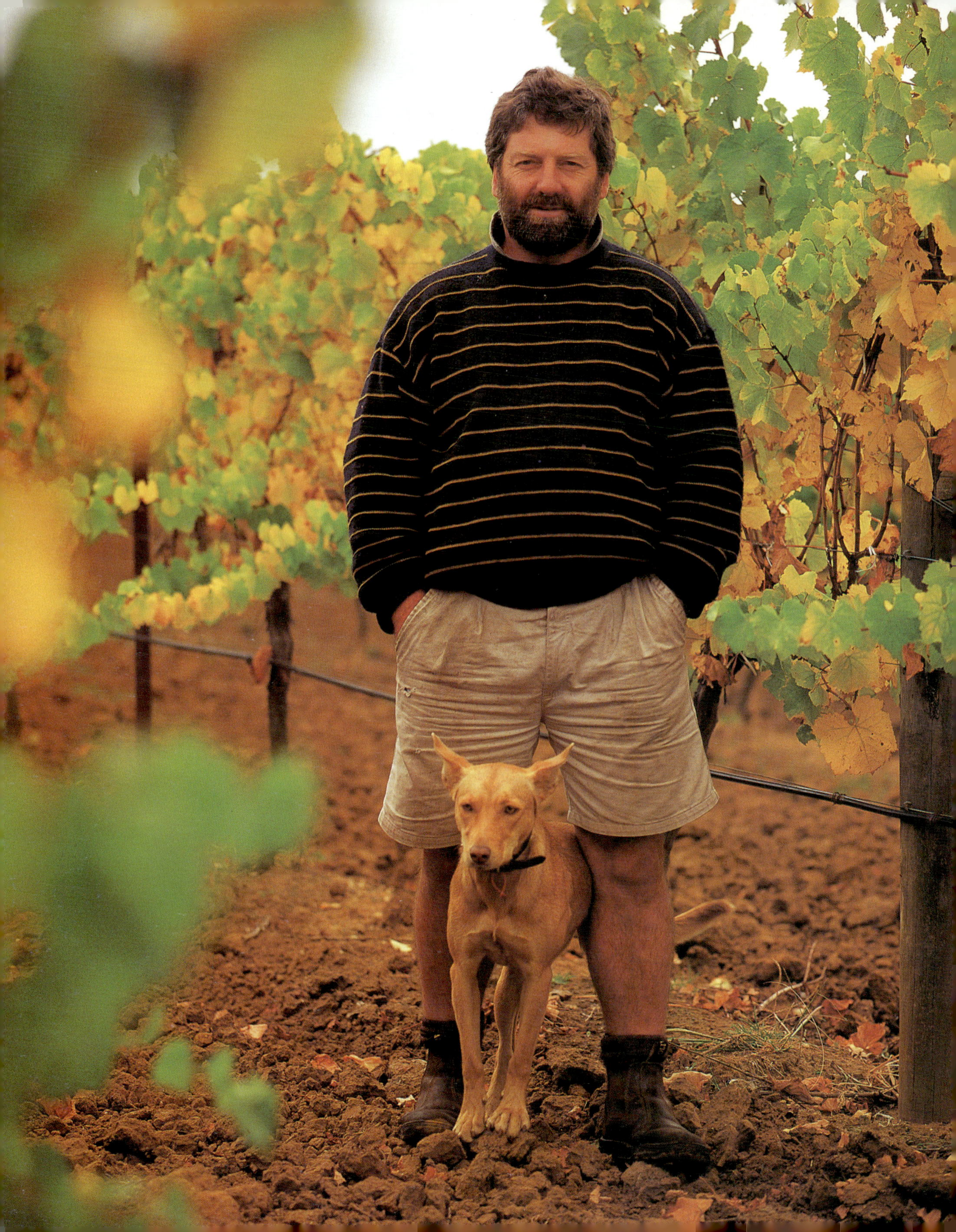

and Sunbury and the Mornington Peninsula) enjoy. There are undoubtedly some great winemakers and vineyards in the area — and they are profiled here — but the region is a long way off returning to its nineteenth-century glory.

Partly this has been the result of small-scale winemaking, less-than-wonderful viticulture, and a reticence among some winemakers to band together for a greater cause — all a result in turn of the fact that Geelong and the Bellarine had — and still has — comparatively few vineyards.

But perhaps this is changing. More and more people are planting. Cellar doors and wineries are under construction. And for the last two years, the Geelong Winegrowers' Association has held an inter-regional mini-wine show, where outside wine judges (myself included) have been asked to assess the entries, award prizes for excellence and help place the wines in a wider competitive context.

Hopefully, all this can only lead to a better range of better wines being made in the region. And if, as George Biron puts it, 'the pioneers of the wine industry undoubtedly provide the nucleus around which the regional food producers can develop', then that is good news for everybody.

Bannockburn

In very early 1998, a few weeks before vintage was due to begin, a dark and brutal hailstorm swept through the Bannockburn vineyards just off the Midland Highway, north-west of Geelong. It was as though the storm knew what it was looking for: paddocks on either side remained untouched while the barrage of icy stones destroyed the majority of the nearly-ripe grapes. As if this wasn't enough, 1998 was shaping up to be a cracking vintage. And to add insult to injury, the hailstorm came just months after the death of Bannockburn's founder, Stuart Hooper.

Bannockburn winemaker, Gary Farr, didn't waste any time. Grapes needed to be found, and fast. After all, distributors around Australia and around the world were expecting 1998 wines from Bannockburn. If that wine didn't arrive, there were going to be thousands of very upset customers — loyal followers of the vineyard that have tracked its progress over the last twenty years with delicious interest.

Farr was on the phone the next day, scrounging a tonne of chardonnay here, three tonnes of shiraz there, pulling in all the favours he could from his contacts in the wine industry. It is a mark of the respect his peers have for him and the Bannockburn name that he was swamped with offers to help — and swamped with some of the best grapes in Australia.

In August the same year, Farr held a party — sorry, tasting — in his winery, and invited those who had participated in the rescue of Bannockburn 1998 to come and taste what he had done with their grapes. The final Bannockburn wines, made from blends of others' fruit, had already been put together; but Farr had fermented each incoming batch separately, and had kept a couple of bottles of the resulting dozens of wines for this tasting.

The guest list read like a Who's Who of the industry: winemakers and representatives were there from, among others: Tarrawarra, Charles Melton, Taltarni, Dalwhinnie, Murrundindi, Cape Mentelle, Dromana Estate, Henschke and Katnook Estate.

The tasting was fascinating. It gave all those present an opportunity to see what another winemaker — in a couple of cases on the other side of the continent — could, would do with

Left • Gary Farr, among the vines at Bannockburn.

their fruit. In Gary Farr's case, it gave him an unparalleled opportunity to compare his fruit with some of the best from elsewhere — and to try and work out what makes it different.

And the conclusions? There is no doubt in my mind that the quality and style of Bannockburn's three top wines in a hail-free year — the chardonnay, pinot noir and shiraz — are due in roughly equal measure to the specific qualities of the grapes he grows (due in turn to the *terroir* or soil, climate and environment of the vines at Bannockburn) and the skills of the winemaker.

I say this because the single batch samples, while distinctively Farr-made — not squeaky clean, using techniques picked up on his many trips to Burgundy to work vintage with the celebrated Jacques Seysses at Domaine Dujac — still had clear regional and vineyard characters poking through: mintiness in one Pyrenees pinot noir, for example, and rich pineapple flavours in one Margaret River chardonnay.

At the same time, the finished wines Farr had blended together from these disparate elements tasted uncannily like Bannockburn wines: elegant, fine chardonnay, tight, dark, reserved pinot, spicy, taut shiraz. Regional characters had been subjugated to a house style.

That house style is quite European, and very influenced by Farr's time in Burgundy. Since the 1980s he has been using Burgundian methods such as barrel-fermenting chardonnay; fermenting wines using 'wild' or ambient rather than cultured, inoculated yeasts; and close-planting pinot noir at 3000 vines for approximately every half a hectare, rather than the usual 1000, resulting in hugely concentrated wine.

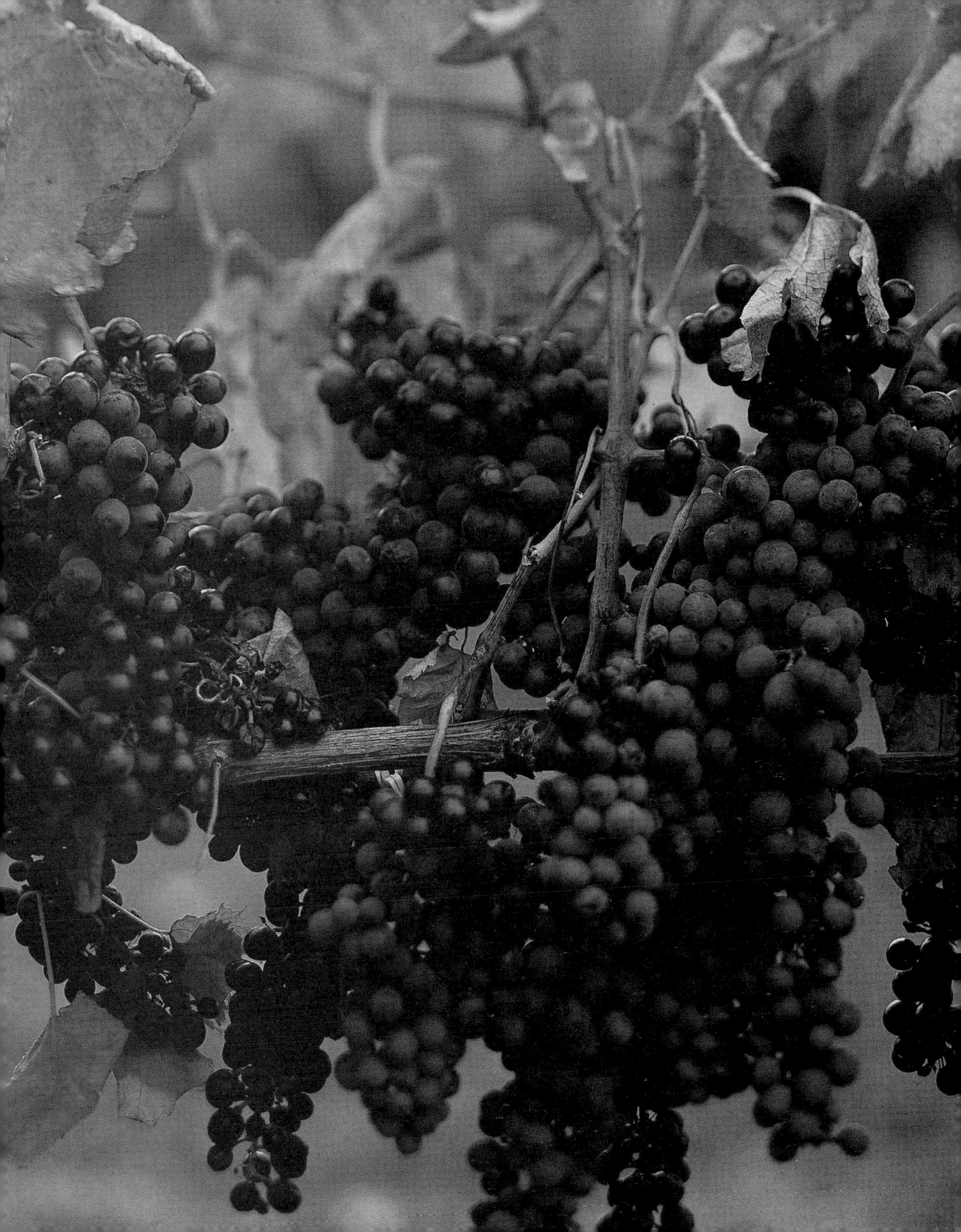

And, since 1991, his shiraz has changed radically — from big and earthy to spicy and fruity — thanks to the influence of Rhône winemaker Alain Graillot, himself influenced by Seysses. Other wines are also made, including a cabernet merlot, a sauvignon blanc and a gently pink wine called saignée, made from juice bled off from a vat of fermenting red grapes, but the top three are still the top three.

Gary Farr is often described as the grumpiest winemaker in Australia. He can certainly be brusque. There is no cellar door at Bannockburn Vineyards — some would say, more to protect the public from Gary rather than protecting Gary from the public. But a more accurate way of describing him would be blunt, straightforward, no-bullshit — refreshingly so, especially in a wine world increasingly bogged down in hype, bottom-lines and spectacular amounts of bullshit.

A couple of years ago, Bannockburn released the first vintages of two ultra-premium wines, SRH chardonnay (the initals of Bannockburn's founder) and the serrée pinot noir (serrée means close-planted) at around the $100-a-bottle mark. Both were tiny commercial releases of special wines that, up to that point, had been reserved for personal consumption by the Farr and Hooper families, as well as for getting wine writers drunk on — one of the fondest and most bizarre wine memories I have is sitting in the little old fibro shack in the middle of the original Bannockburn shiraz block, eating frankfurters and drinking the 1989 serrée out of big Reidel glasses.

But that's not the point. The point is this: other Australian wines have been released during the last decade at close to or exceeding the hundred buck mark, and most of those releases have been accompanied by breathless, reverential hype. Gary Farr's attitude it seemed to me was more along the lines of: well I reckon they're worth it and if you don't then you can bugger off, because I'll drink it all myself anyway. Blunt, straightforward, honest.

Having spent a bit of time with Gary Farr over the years, at tastings, dinners and in the winery, and having got past the grumpy outer shell, I find there's also a big streak of generosity about the man. Just go back to that tasting of his 1998 wines: as well as organising lunch for everybody (a sublimely brilliant duck stew cooked by Walter Bourke of Walters Wine Bar), Gary also opened ten vintages of Domaine Dujac burgundies as an extra treat.

The word 'bacchic' springs to mind. As he said at the time, any excuse to have a party.

Prince Albert

I asked Bruce Hyett (left) why he decided to plant vines on almost all of his two-hectare property at Waurn Ponds a quarter of a century ago. And why he chose to plant only pinot noir. He rummaged around in his desk and brought out a long piece of card with a panoramic compo-site photograph assembled on it.

The photographic panorama was taken by Hyett from the top of the hill looking down at the most famous red wine (therefore pinot noir) vineyards in Burgundy: Romanée Conti, Vosne Romanée, Romanée St Vivant. And just off to the left of the panorama was another photograph that looked as though it should have been part of the larger picture: exactly the same soil, exactly the same aspect, uncanny resemblance.

'That's our vineyard,' said Hyett. 'That's why.' And nothing more needed to be said.

Standing at the top of the fine north-facing slope that is the Prince Albert Vineyard, you can see why David Pettavel decided to plant there in 1857 and why Hyett replanted in 1975. It is a suntrap, with wonderful red soil over limestone: the perfect pinot noir site. You can also see why it was chosen for a visit by Prince Alfred, son of Albert, in 1867: in its (much larger) heyday, with a working splendid winery and residence, it must have been one of the region's showpieces.

The vineyard is run on organic principles, and all the wine is made by Hyett in a small but functional winery on the property. No wine is brought in from elsewhere (it has been occasionally in the past, but not for years), and consequently, the quality of the 600 or so cases produced annually can suffer the slings and arrows of outrageous vintage conditions.

But when it is good — best years include 1992, 1994, 1997 and 1998 — Prince Albert pinot noir is lovely: silky, rich and deep. A glimpse, perhaps, of what Geelong wine tasted like in its first golden age.

The wine shops of Geelong

Browsing through good wine shops is one of my favourite pastimes. Poring over old bottles, ferreting out wine bargains, staring at the unaffordable, drooling over the exotic. I love it. Actually getting round to buying stuff is often secondary to the hours of 'just looking' that precede it. I've done a lot of poring, ferreting, staring and drooling in Geelong because it has more than its fair share of groggeries. And if you're heading down the Road and you're not happy drinking Jacobs Creek or cold beer, I suggest you visit them on the way, because although there are some good retail wine outlets on the Road — the Warrnambool Hotel is one — they are few and far between.

If the chaotic, old-fashioned style of wine shop appeals to you, head to Neuschafers in Mercer Street. It's the bottle shop with the sacks of onions outside, you can't miss it. And it is stuffed to the gills with crates of wine — the inside looks like a particularly chaotic Dr Seuss illustration, with piles of booze threatening to topple at any moment and bring the whole lot down with them. It's mostly currently available stuff, but older vintages — especially of fortified wine — occasionally surface. Prices are great, even if storage conditions aren't. It's a trade-off.

Far more organised and, for me, far more enticing, is Bannockburn Cellars in Pakington Street. This is simply one of the best wine shops in the country. As well as keen pricing and a wonderful range of local, Australian and imported wines, there are terrific cleanskins and older vintages of wines many Melbourne wine shops would love to get their hands on. Bannockburn Cellars was run by Bruce Pollard (above) when the first edition of this book was published, but Randall has since opened a new wine store called Randall the Wine Merchant at the other end of Pakington Street.

Bannockburn Cellars was set up by Bannockburn Vineyard's Stuart Hooper, who had bought the Chas Cole licence, which itself stretched back to well before the turn of the century. A few years ago, Pollard revived the old Chas Cole name and started bottling wine under a label that featured the original Chas Cole bluestone building.

Another shop was established with the Chas Cole name — on the Princes Highway heading out of Geelong towards the Great Ocean Road. It is unmissable. Again, the range is pretty good, but the big attraction is the fact that the far end of the shop is taken up by a wall of barrels, full of slowly maturing fortified wines sourced from around the country (with an emphasis, as there should be, on Rutherglen and McLaren Vale).

It is a mouth-watering slice of history.

Scotchmans Hill

I don't quite know how I managed it, but I sped right past the rather prominent 'Scotchmans Hill Vineyard' sign that guides you off Scotchmans Road into the cellar door car park when I drove down there last. It's a pretty big vineyard — the biggest in the area — and the cellar door is one of the region's most frequented so missing it is actually quite hard. No, I know how I missed it. I was looking in the opposite direction at the stunning view across the bay towards Melbourne, glimmering greyly in the distance.

This part of the Bellarine Peninsula is really quite picturesque, in a black chocolatey soil, windswept old trees and increasing numbers of regimented vine rows kind of way. You can see how David Browne fell in love with the place as a boy on family holidays in Portarlington. And you can understand why, when the Scotchmans Hill property came up for sale in 1975, Browne, by then a young successful stockbroker, decided to buy it.

The first three hectares or so went in in 1982, with around another 17 hectares going in the following year. Today the Scotchmans Hill Vineyard group comprises 66 hectares of its own vineyards and another 100 from contract growers. Last year 12,000 cases of wine were made here, but that is set to increase dramatically. When I finally managed to find the place, I discovered a building site. With a spanking new barrel store already up, a roofless tank farm half-way through construction and the old winery about to be remodelled, I was greeted not by the sound of gentle bubbling fermentation but by jackhammers and fork-lifts.

This expansion comes as no surprise. From the beginning, Scotchmans Hill has always been run very professionally, with a firm eye to making both good wine and lots of money. The Browne family are thoroughly involved, with David and his wife, Vivienne, running the show, their son Matthew acting as assistant winemaker, and other son Andrew, just back from a stint in the UK wine-trade and very keen to get into the marketing side of things.

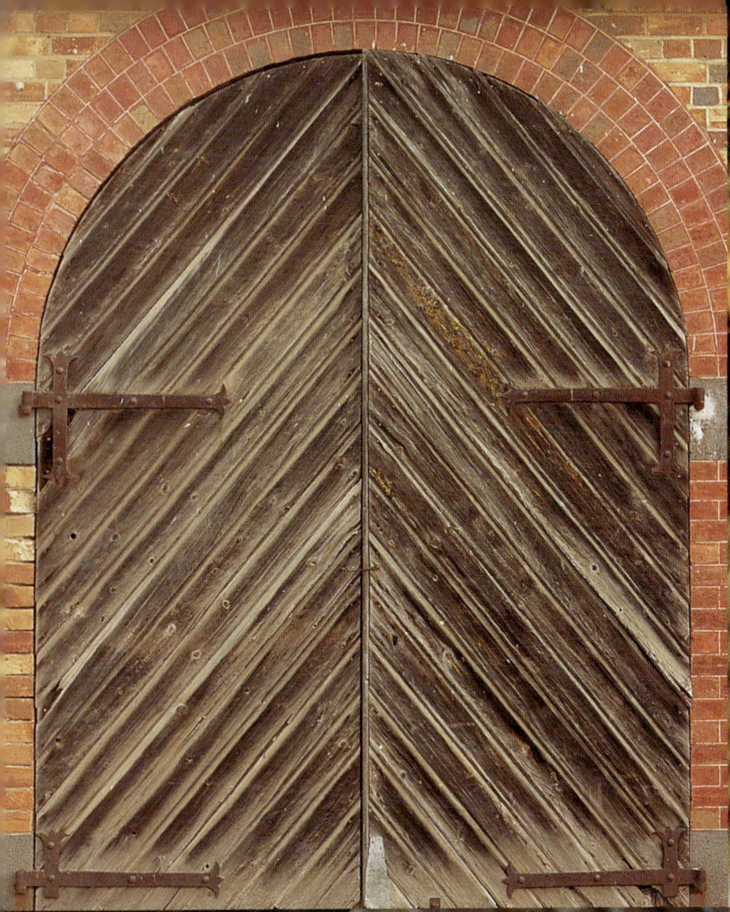

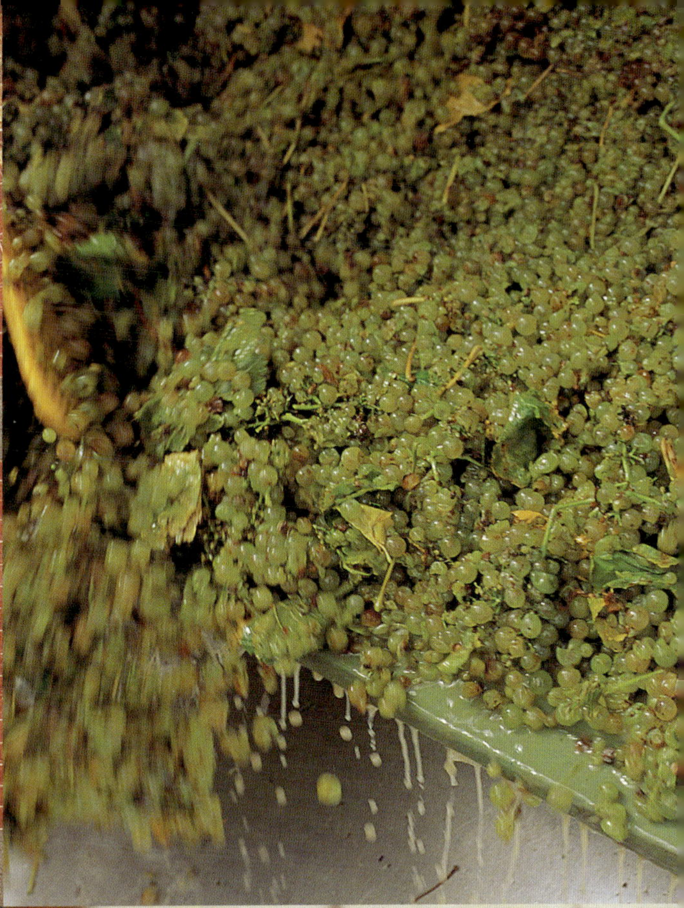

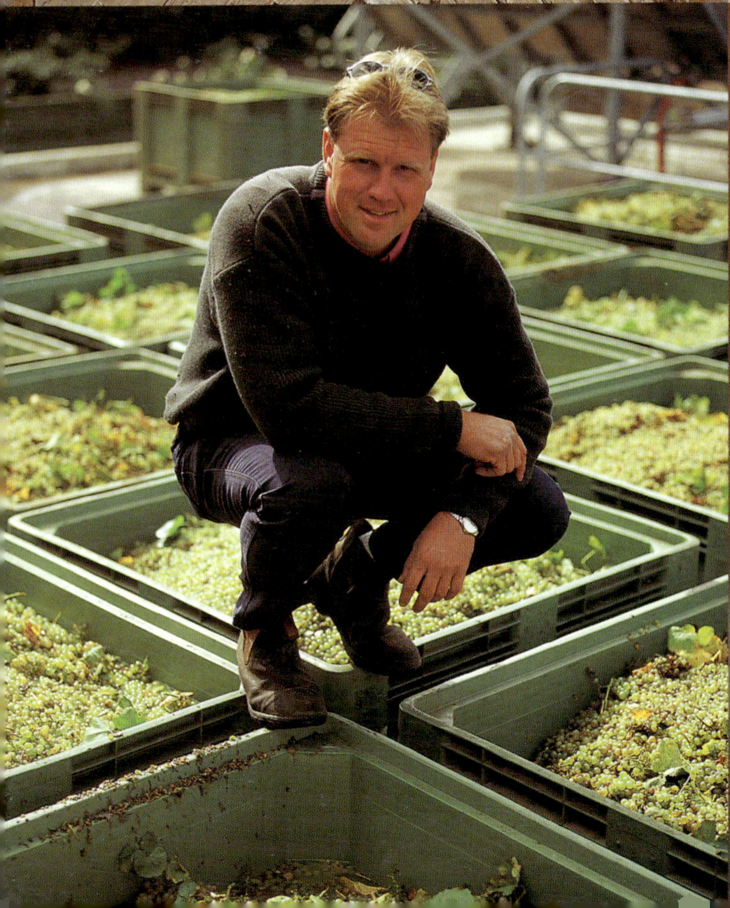

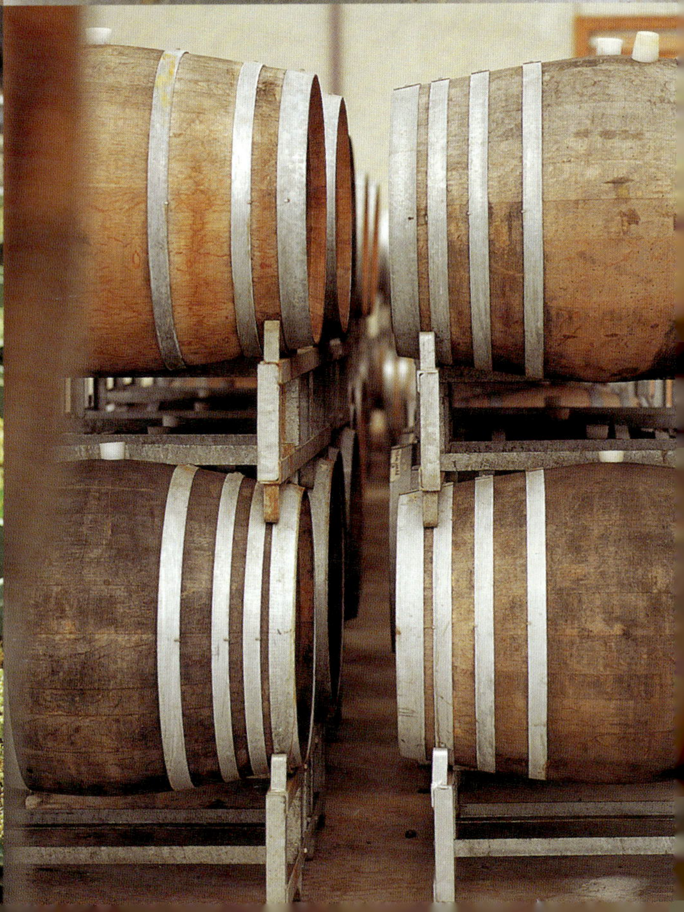

Winemaker Robin Brockett was lured from New Zealand in 1988, and has made some of the most reliable wines in the region ever since. But Brockett is acutely aware that while a reputation for commercial success and reliability is one thing, a reputation for making wines of character, longevity and greatness is another.

He takes me on a tour of the vineyards already established atop this old extinct volcano to show me the immaculate viticulture. As we sweep down a gully and frighten a white horse drinking from a dam, he points out a new block of shiraz: up to now, pinot noir has been Scotchmans' big volume red wine, but in the warmer, sheltered sites, shiraz may yet prove a goer. Echoes of times past?

We then head across to Spray Farm, the remarkable 1860s homestead purchased by the Browne family a few years ago and in the slow process of restoration. This will, one day soon, be one of the most remarkable conference venues in Australia — the front doors open to an unparalleled sweeping view of Geelong, the You Yangs and Melbourne across the bay. In the meantime, it is a spectacular venue for an annual music festival.

Some Spray Farm wines are already produced — simpler, more fruit-driven, cheaper than the Scotchmans Hill wines — from fruit grown elsewhere in the region. Still, one day the property may also yield some great wine from the vines that have only recently started bearing fruit.

And then we head back up to the Brownes' house overlooking the original Scotchmans Hill vineyard for a tasting. Brockett wants to show me how well his wines age, and how many people were wrong to dismiss them as 'commercial', fly-by-night products.

We start with a dry, minerally 1998 sauvignon blanc, one of the big sellers for Scotchmans, and a wonderful accompaniment to the local seafood (the voice of much experience talking: this wine appears to be on every restaurant list from here to Portland). We end with a 1996 cabernet merlot which, while nice, is also slightly herbaceous and stalky — which in turn only reconfirms my opinion that this area is simply too cool for the late-ripening cabernet to flourish.

But the wines we taste in the middle — a deliciously complex, toasty, fine chardonnay and deep, smoky, juicy pinot noir, both from the 1994 vintage — make Brockett's point loud and clear. Sure, they're not ancient and venerable, but they're certainly not simple, drink-now wines.

With both feet firmly placed on the ground, Brockett is also beginning to refine his winemaking in other ways than simply ensuring their longevity. He's experimenting with wild yeast fermentation (and he's encouraged by the extra complexities it's giving him), and he's looking to keep separate small parcels from the older, established and better vineyards for special, reserve releases.

Scotchmans Hill certainly looks set to achieve that rare double in the next few years: getting bigger as well as getting better.

Clockwise from left • Wine stored in barrels at Scotchmans Hill. Winemaker Robin Brockett. Spray Farm. Chardonnay grapes.

More than wine

Wine, of course, is by no means the only alcoholic drink to have been produced in this part of the world over the last century and a half. Both beer and spirits have, at various times and in varying levels of legitimacy, been hugely important industries to the people of Geelong and the Great Ocean Road.

Wherever Australians gather together — be they early pioneering settlers, footy supporters, business people or pensioners — alcohol is likely to be involved. So it's no surprise to learn that brewing officially began in Geelong in 1841, with the Volum brewery becoming a vast affair, selling out to the Ballarat Brewing Company in the 1950s and to CUB in 1958.

From the 1920s to the 1980s, and reaching a high-point in the '50s and '60s, Geelong was also home to the Corio Distillery, the southern hemisphere's largest producer of spirits. Older readers may remember with a mixture of affection and fear the famous Corio brand of whisky.

There are also wonderful stories of illicit stills and sly-grog shops popping up all the way along the Great Ocean Road, as settlements were formed and people became thirsty from chopping down all those trees. The most infamous was at Distillery Creek, near Aireys Inlet: an inordinate number of funerals were reported in the area, the coffins containing moonshine rather than cadavers. This particular moonshine was popular as far as Port Fairy.

Most of the brewing and distilling traditions of the region are lost, but the Steam Packet Brewing Company keeps an essence of it alive at the Scottish Chiefs Tavern tucked away down narrow Corio Street in the centre of Geelong. This popular pub caters mostly to a young, band-watching crowd, but a few beers are also produced on-site in the cute glassed-in brewery: of the range, the Stoker's Ale tickled my fancy most, with its porter-like mild bitterness and roasted barley flavours.

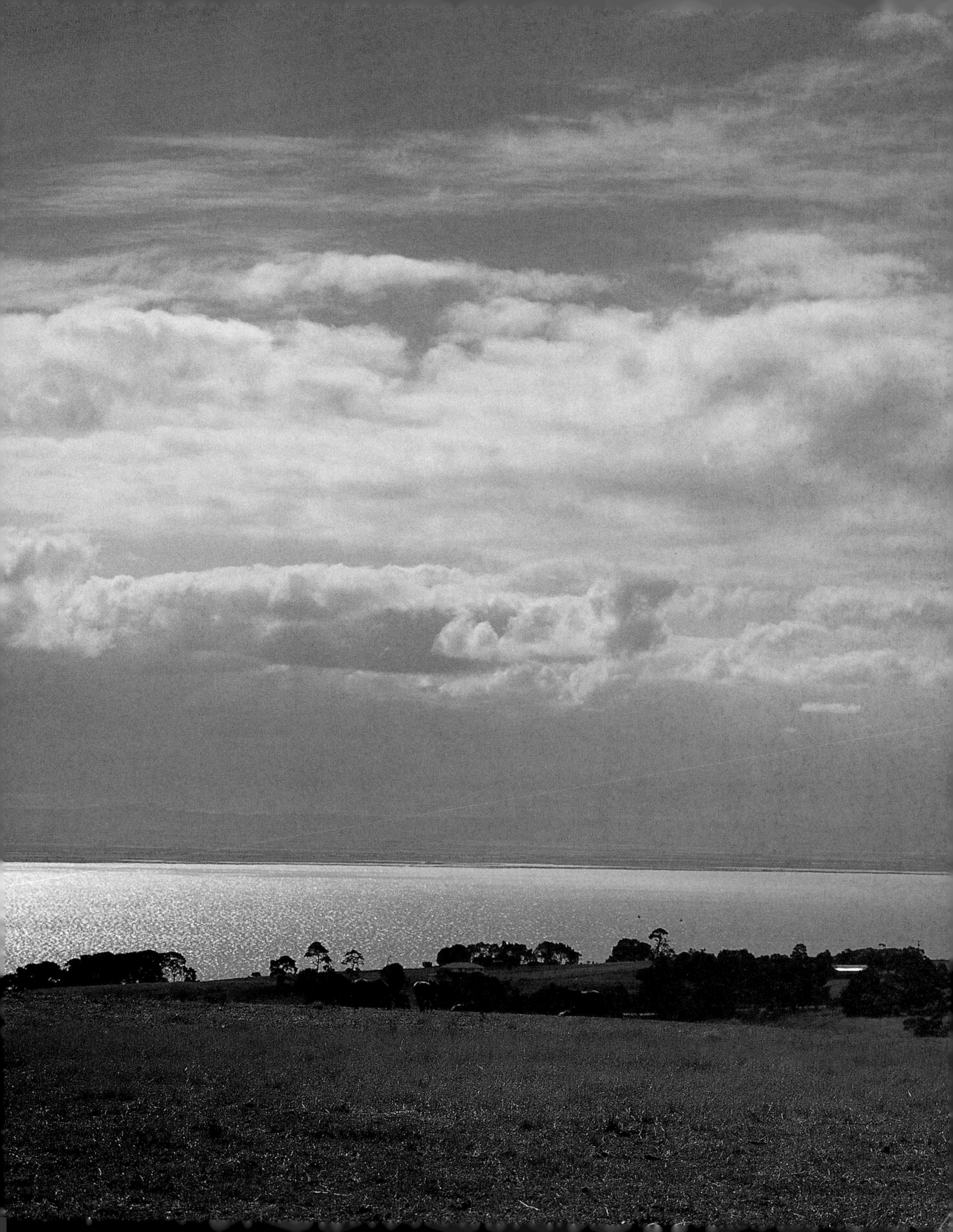

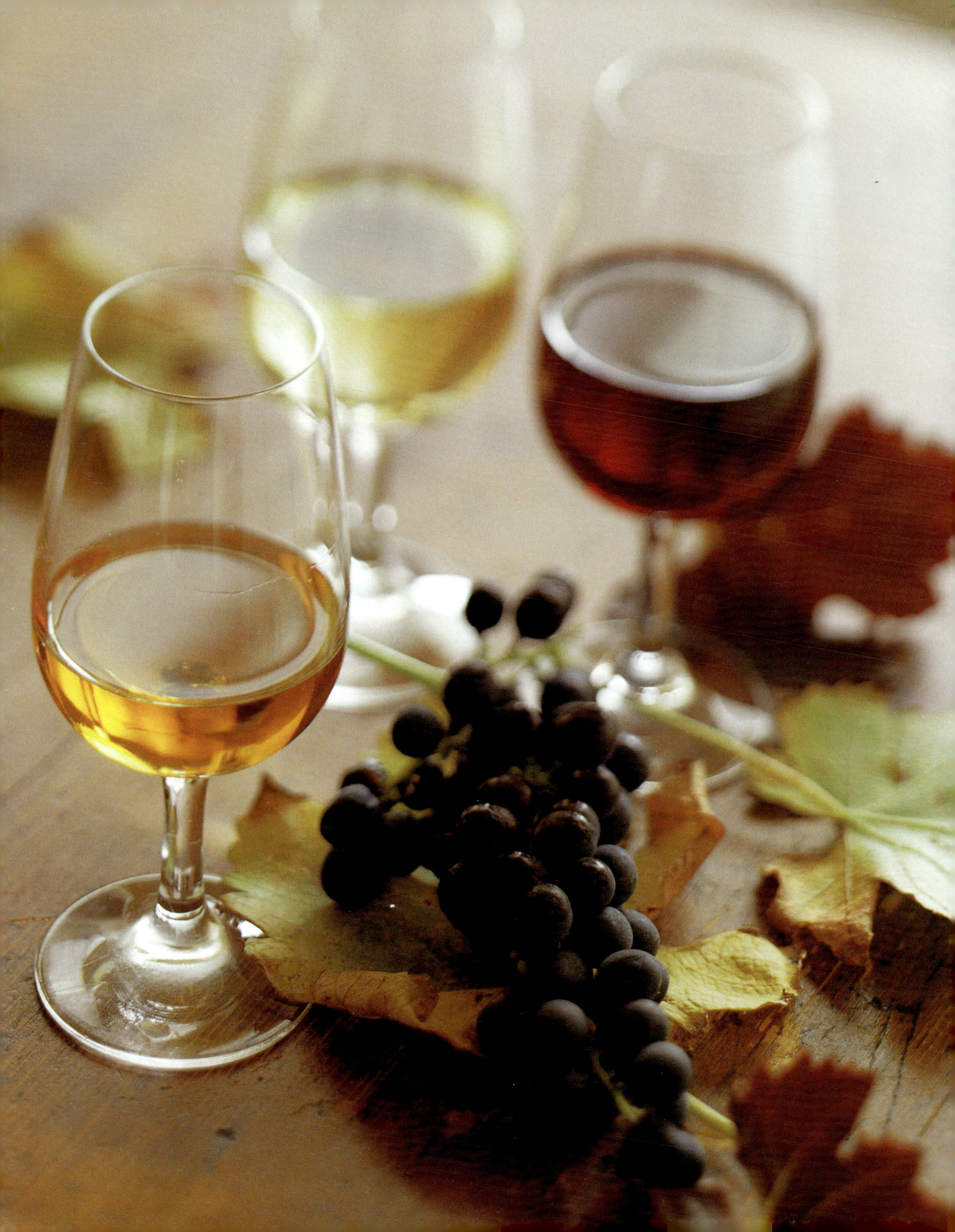

The far south-west

The light is fading, the sun has given up for the day, and the cold air is beginning to bite. I'm at the bottom of a wet, fertile and slightly overgrown garden, snipping asparagus spears from their bed of straw with an antique bone-handled knife. The garden runs down from a mostly Edwardian homestead belonging to the Thomson family, who have farmed their large, wide, windswept station at Crawford River in remote south-western Victoria since the 1870s. The asparagus bed is ninety years old.

John Thomson's asparagus-snipping technique leaves me for dead. He's scything whole bunches while I manage to step on more than I harvest. He's snipping while he talks in his passionate, rapid-fire way about the things he loves: the sheep he runs on his family's large farm (including an old English fat lamb breed called Lincoln — they used to use its fleece for judges' wigs); the shocking price of wool these days; and how the vineyard he established on one north-facing bit of his property in 1975 became much more than just a hobby a long time ago.

He's insistent about this last bit. Because of Crawford River's great distance from most wine writers, it is viewed by them as a hobby operation. Which is a great contrast to the list, proudly displayed on the cellar door, of restaurants in Melbourne and Sydney that stock Crawford River wines. It reads like a Who's Who of the best and the trendiest. Another example of the wine-scribbling fraternity being slightly out of step with the wine-buying population.

Half an hour or so later and we're tucking into the freshly harvested green spears, now piping hot and drizzled with olive oil. The kitchen is one of many big, rambling rooms in the homestead. John and his wife Cathy sleep in the 1850s bluestone bit which dates back to the time when 36,000 hectares of land were owned by the one family. The formal lounge room (circa 1910) is full of Edwardian memorabilia: one of Cathy Thomson's ancestors was Ernest 'Chinese' Morrison, the journalist who made his name by walking from Queenscliff to Adelaide along the coast when he was seventeen, and publishing his diary in a Melbourne newspaper.

On the kitchen table are some bottles of Thomson's Crawford River whites: stunningly tangy, juicy, incisive riesling and a crisp, fresh, reserved blend of sauvignon blanc and semillon. Thomson is well known for making these two styles, especially the riesling. It is one of Australia's best examples of the grape variety, but its perceived remoteness from an established wine region (it's actually only a couple of hours' drive from Coonawarra) means it often gets overlooked when the riesling roll-call is recited. Indeed, even though increasing numbers are beginning to plant in this flat, broad, Panavision-scale country near the old whaling-town of Portland (fifteen vineyards and 800 tonnes of grapes estimated for the 1999 vintage), the area in general is often overlooked.

Which is understandable but a shame, because apart from Crawford River's twenty-five year pedigree, there are others who can provide historical depth here.

Karl Seppelt, of the South Australian winemaking family firm, first planted in the region at Drumborg in 1964, the year after he'd pioneered Padthaway, to the north of Coonawarra over the South Australian border. He envisaged the region's really quite cool climate as being perfect for sparkling and aromatic whites, and planted big.

That vision was certainly realised: Seppelt's Drumborg riesling is exceptional and extraordinarily long lived, while the chardonnay and pinot noir from Drumborg is much prized by Seppelt sparkling winemakers in their blends. Occasionally, too, a deep, ripe Drumborg pinot noir still wine is released; and, with bottle age, Seppelt's single vineyard Drumborg sparklings are among the best in Australia. The late-ripening red grape cabernet sauvignon was planted here and is persisted with by Seppelt but seldom reaches the heights of John Thomson's (just like at Scotchmans Hill, I still can't understand why Seppelt don't make more of the earlier-ripening and more reliable merlot).

Recently, Seppelt have expanded their vineyards at Drumborg to include the spicy, fairly full-flavoured white wine variety, pinot gris. Early results are very encouraging: savoury-finishing but fruity and highly gluggable. It will be a while, though, before riesling is toppled as the number one white variety in the area — especially if Barretts and Kingsley, two vineyards established a little further south near Portland in the early '80s persist in turning out the odd good dry riesling and occasionally exceptional sweet riesling made from fruit affected by the noble rot, botrytis cinerea.

But back to the kitchen. Cathy Thomson rescues a large shoulder of recently home-slaughtered lamb from the wood-burning oven and John pours a glass of his 1994 cabernet sauvignon. My rational, sceptical mind tries feebly to resist, but one sip, one mouthful and I'm off on a private rave about the rightness, the beauty and the sheer pleasure of the true regional food and wine match.

The way that the elegant, pure, supple berry fruit of the cabernet — perfectly poised, not a tad herbaceous, as you might expect from this part of the world — floods over and into the tender sweetness of the lamb in your mouth. The way the clean acidity of the wine cuts the fattiness of the meat, creating a sensory combination that is more wonderful than the sum of its parts. Surely, I think, there has to be some perfect significance in the fact that these two things were grown on the same ridge of rough purple sandy soil. Doesn't there?

I come back to earth and find that John and Cathy Thomson aren't laughing. In fact, they are nodding in agreement. Which means one of two things. Either we're right, or we're all as loopy as each other. But who cares? I pour another glass of wine, heap up another plateful of meat. And I sleep deeply and contented in Crawford River that night.

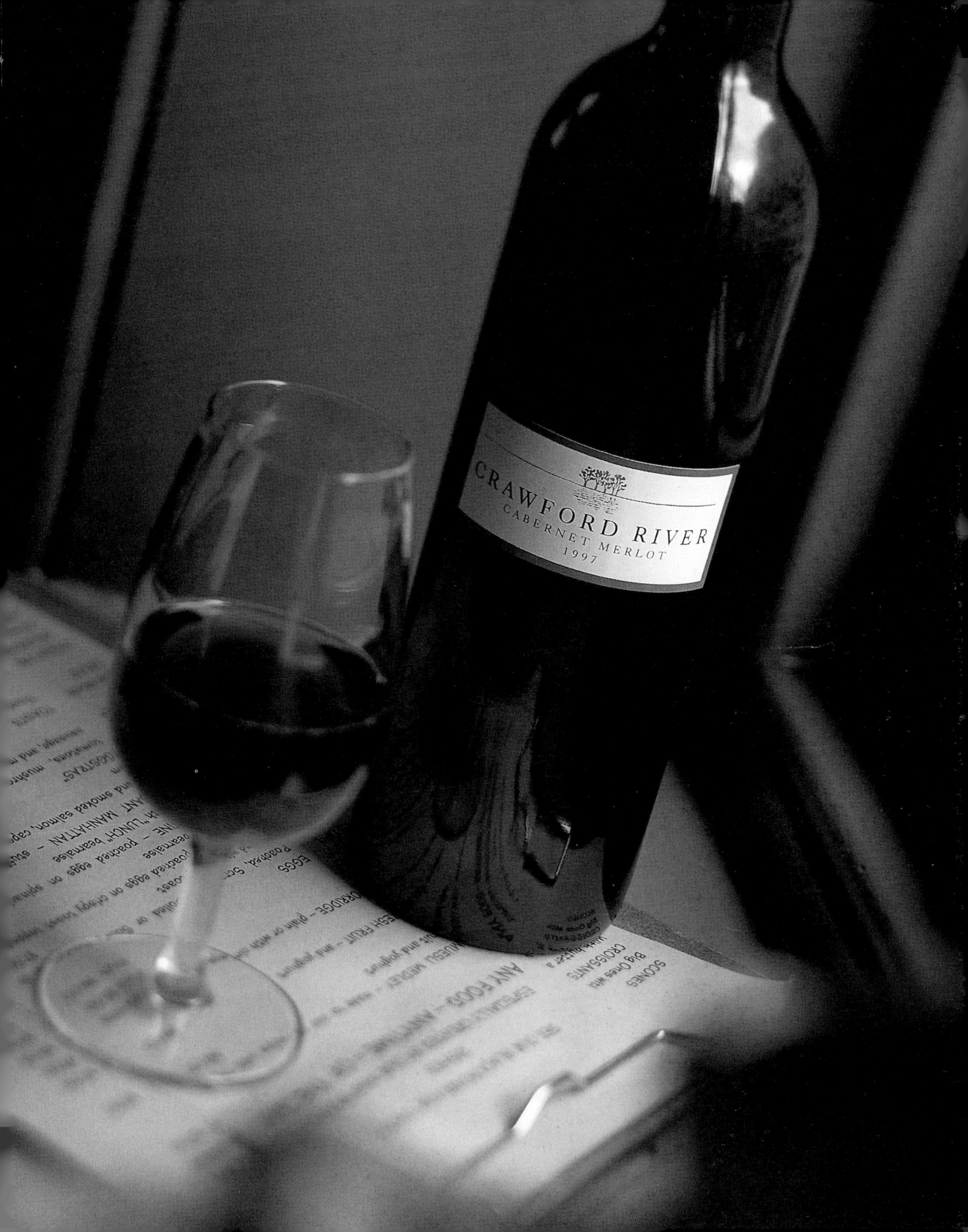
CRAWFORD RIVER
CABERNET MERLOT
1997

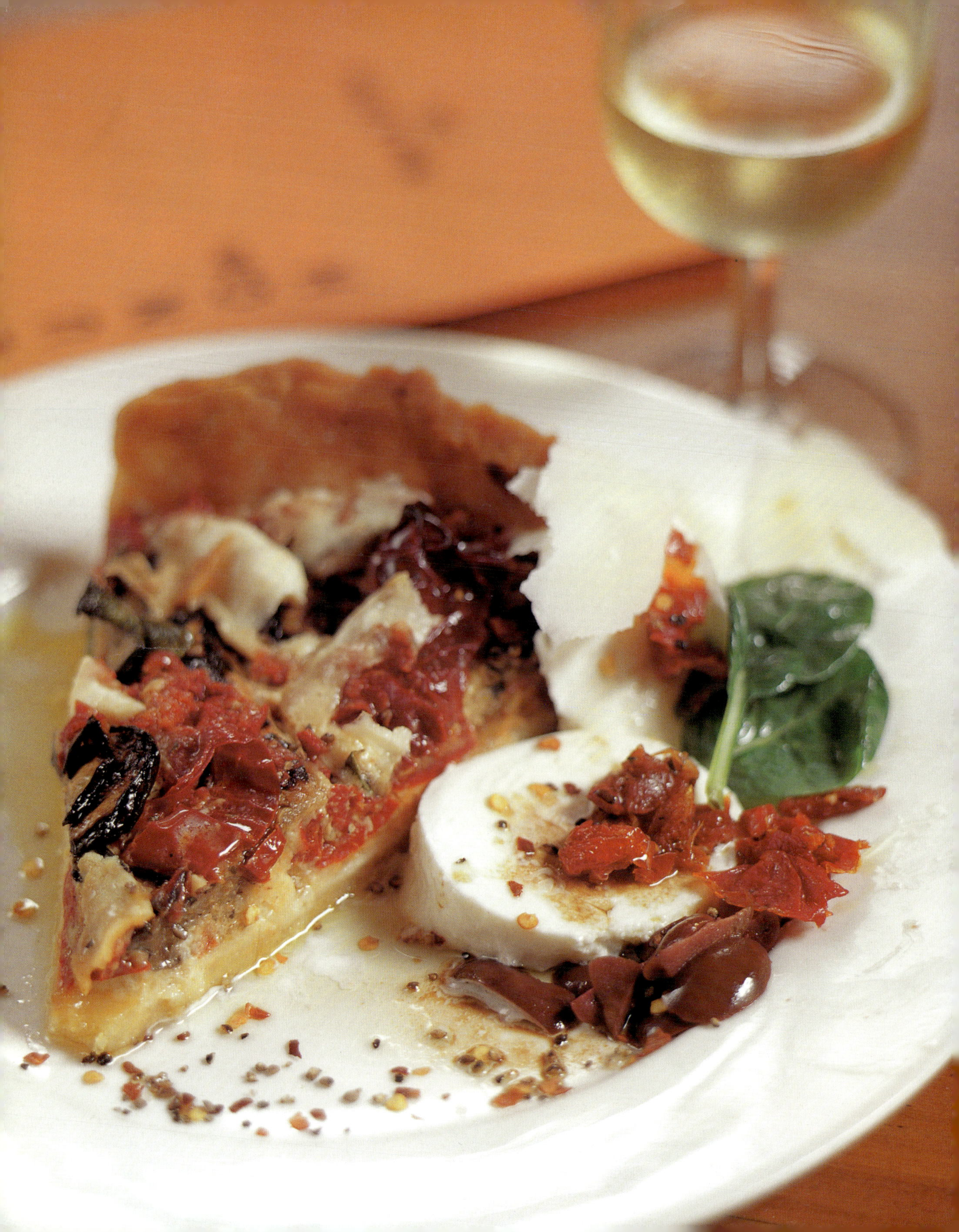

After the vintage

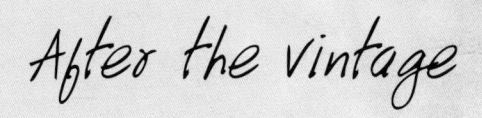

A Tart of Grilled Vegetables
and Shaw River Mozzarella

Pork with Butter Beans

Quince Puddings with Vanilla
Custard and Quince Syrup

The Recovery
Greek Egg and Lemon Soup

A Tart of Grilled Vegetables and Shaw River Mozzarella

Lunch, Port Fairy

Serves 6-8

Pastry

2 ½ cups plain flour
pinch of salt
180 g chilled butter, diced
2 eggs

Put all ingredients in food processor and mix quickly until it forms a ball. Wrap in plastic and refrigerate for 10 minutes. Roll out on a floured bench and put in a large springform tin (24 cm diameter x 6 cm high).

Freeze for 30 minutes. Blind bake for 20 minutes, then remove weights and bake for a further 10 minutes.

Filling

2 Spanish onions, sliced
butter for frying
2 eggs
½ cup cream
cracked black pepper and salt to taste
5 thick slices charred eggplant
2 whole capsicum, charred, peeled and sliced
10 oven-dried tomatoes
3 artichokes, charred and sliced
3 balls Shaw River mozzarella, sliced
½ cup shaved Parmesan

Fry onion slices in a little butter until soft and slightly brown.

Lightly beat eggs, cream, pepper and salt. Put ⅔ of this in pastry shell. Add all other ingredients, then top with remaining egg/cream mixture. Bake in a moderate oven until firm (30-40 minutes).

Serve at room temperature, garnished with fine slices of mozzarella, oven-dried tomatoes, pitted black olives and a drizzle of balsamic vinegar with olive oil. Dust with cracked black pepper.

Pork with Butter Beans

Gail Thomas, food journalist

This is a Spanish dish, from Asturia, known as *Fabada Asturiana*.

Serves 8

1 kg butter beans (or small haricot beans)
1 onion, quartered
½ cup olive oil
125 g sliced fat pork
250 g sliced rib of pork
125 g lean pork
250 g sliced chorizo sausage
250 g black pudding (blood sausage)
pinch saffron and salt

Soak beans overnight. Drain, place in pan and cover with water.

Bring to the boil, add onion and oil, then other ingredients, except saffron and salt.

Pound saffron in a mortar with a pinch of salt, dilute with a little water and add to beans. Cover pan tightly, simmer for 2- 2½ hours, making sure beans are always covered with liquid. Season with salt when beans are tender.

Quince Puddings with Vanilla Custard and a Quince Syrup

Sawyers Arms Tavern, Geelong

To Cook Quinces

4 quinces

½ cup sugar

2 cinnamon sticks

vanilla bean

Place the quinces in a saucepan and cover completely with water. Add sugar, cinnamon sticks and vanilla bean.

Cook until a deep pink in colour, approximately 3-4 hours. Make sure quinces are always covered with water.

Quince Syrup

Strain off the liquid from cooking the quinces and place in a pot. Reduce until thick and syrupy.

Quince Puddings

125 g unsalted butter

250 g caster sugar

4 eggs

500 g self-raising flour

1 tsp baking powder

20 ml quince syrup

½ cup milk

4 cooked quinces, peeled and chopped into 1cm dice

Cream butter and sugar until light and creamy. Add eggs one at a time.

Lightly fold in half the flour and baking powder, then milk, syrup and rest of the flour, then the quince flesh. Pour into greased tea cups and place into steamer. Cover with greaseproof paper and lid. Steam for 30-35 minutes.

Vanilla Custard

8 egg yolks

1 cup sugar

4 cups milk

1 soft vanilla bean scraped of its seeds

Combine yolks and sugar. Heat milk with vanilla seeds and bean until just boiling. Pour into egg mix and stir over medium heat until it coats the back of a spoon. 83°C is the exact temperature.

Strain.

Turn out the puddings and serve with the custard and some of the syrup.

THE RECOVERY

Greek Egg and Lemon Soup

Barwon Seafoods, Geelong

Serves 8

2 litres lamb or chicken stock

100 g rice

10 egg yolks

100 ml lemon juice

20 g chopped dill

20 g chopped parsley

salt and pepper

Cook rice in the stock. Mix egg yolks, lemon juice and herbs in a bowl. Pour on a little stock. Add the rest. Reheat until thickened but do not boil. Season and taste.

Serve with crusty white bread.

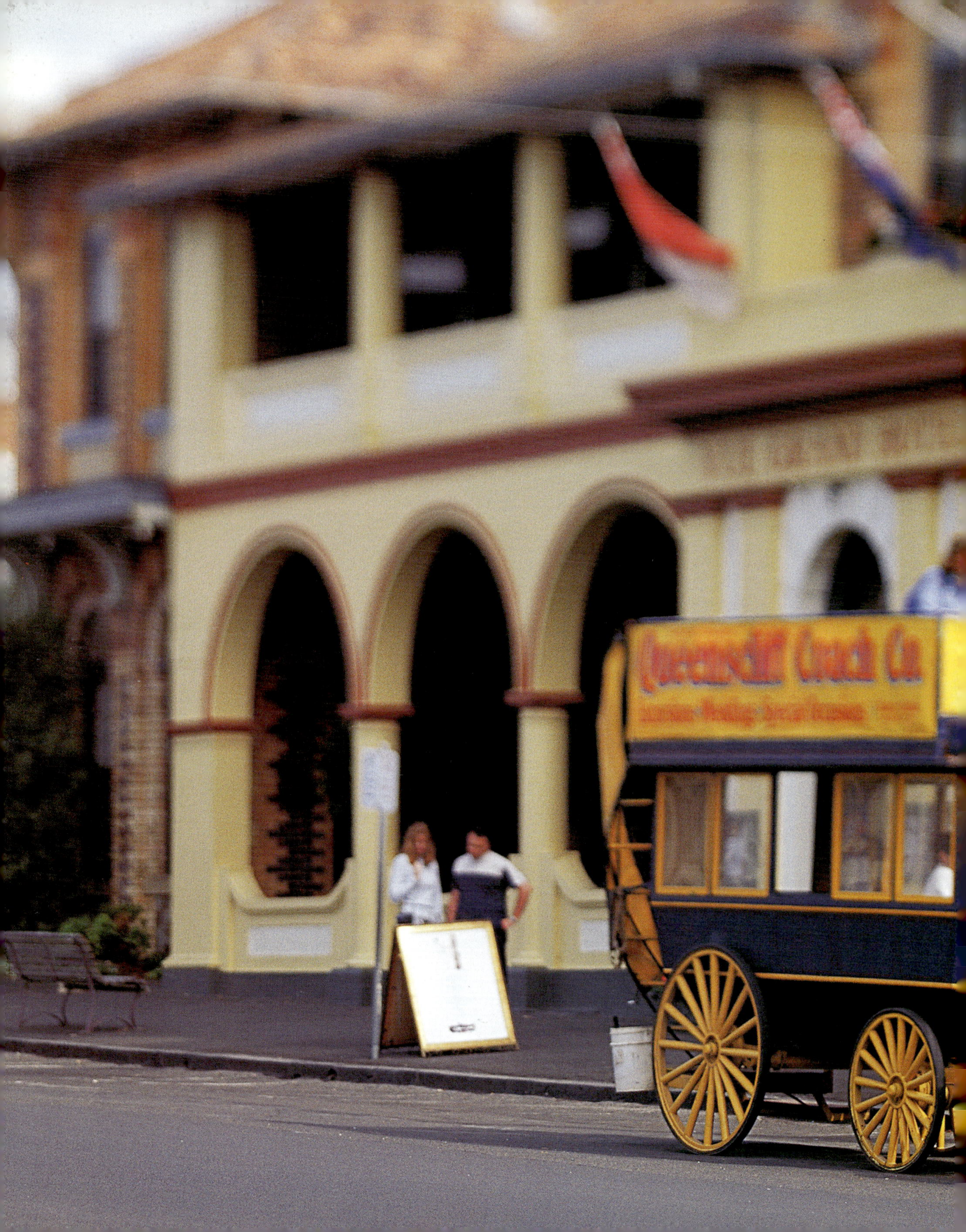
Queenscliff Coach Co

grand old days of queenscliff

Your average Melburnian loves to go on holiday. Just like every other Australian. Try to find a Melburnian to talk to during January, or over Easter or during one of the huge number of long weekends we seem to enjoy. You can't: everybody's down on the beach or up at the snow, or in Queensland.

As soon as the clock strikes 5 pm on the Friday before the holiday officially starts, you can guarantee the roads out of the city will already be packed with cars, groaning under the weight of skis and tents and Eskys and children. Melbourne is still full of people, though. Full of other Australians having their holidays here.

It has always been this way — at least since the Gold Rush of the 1850s. The raucous, muddy, struggling early settlements of Melbourne and Geelong were not even two decades old when little nuggets of the shiny yellow stuff first started popping up out of the ground. Suddenly, some people not only had bags of money to spend, but also — just as alien a feeling — they had bags of free time in which to spend it. A resort was needed, and the little tongue of land called Shortland Bluff, on the western side of the entrance to Port Phillip Bay seemed like just the spot.

Formerly home to a couple of struggling farmers and the odd pilot or two charged with the duty of helping ships navigate the treacherous Rip, the little tongue of land was more attractively renamed Queenscliff in 1853. It soon started drawing in wealthy holiday-makers from the cities across the bay. In 1855, the telegraph from Geelong got through, and the first hotel was erected. The boom had begun.

Over the ensuing thirty years and for a little while after — including during the depression of the 1890s — Queenscliff shimmered as a premier holiday destination. People flocked there, both for health reasons (just think for a second about how grotty early Melbourne must have been) and, increasingly, for social reasons.

The hotels became grander and grander (imagine the battalions of maids and chefs), and the dinners and dances became great social institutions (imagine the stifling discomfort of full dinner dress on a hot January night after one too many glasses of champagne and one too many cigars). Ever-greater numbers of tourists piled off the paddle steamers from Melbourne into those wonderful Victorian inventions, the sea-baths (imagine the weight of your tent-like swimming costume conspiring to drag you to a watery grave). In pictures from this time, the main streets are seething with men in straw boaters, women with parasols and children with stern faces.

The town's fishing industry also grew during this period. Shark, cray and barracouta were hauled onto the jetty at Queenscliff and swiftly transported by rail to Geelong and beyond — as well as straight into waiting pans in the grand hotel kitchens. But after the First World War, both the tourism and fishing industries began a slow fall into decline — the former killed by the closure of the railway and the latter by changing tastes in fish.

Then, about twenty years ago, one by one, those grand hotels began to rumble back to life. Partly as a result, Queenscliff has also been reborn as a premier holiday destination. It is the stories of the three grandest hotels that will be told here.

Mietta's Queenscliff Hotel

We arrived late. It had taken us just a little longer than expected to drive from the Great Ocean Road all the way across the tundra of the Bellarine Peninsula to Queenscliff. There didn't seem to be that much of a hurry, though: cricket on the car radio, sun blazing down from a perfect blue sky. A glorious day for motoring.

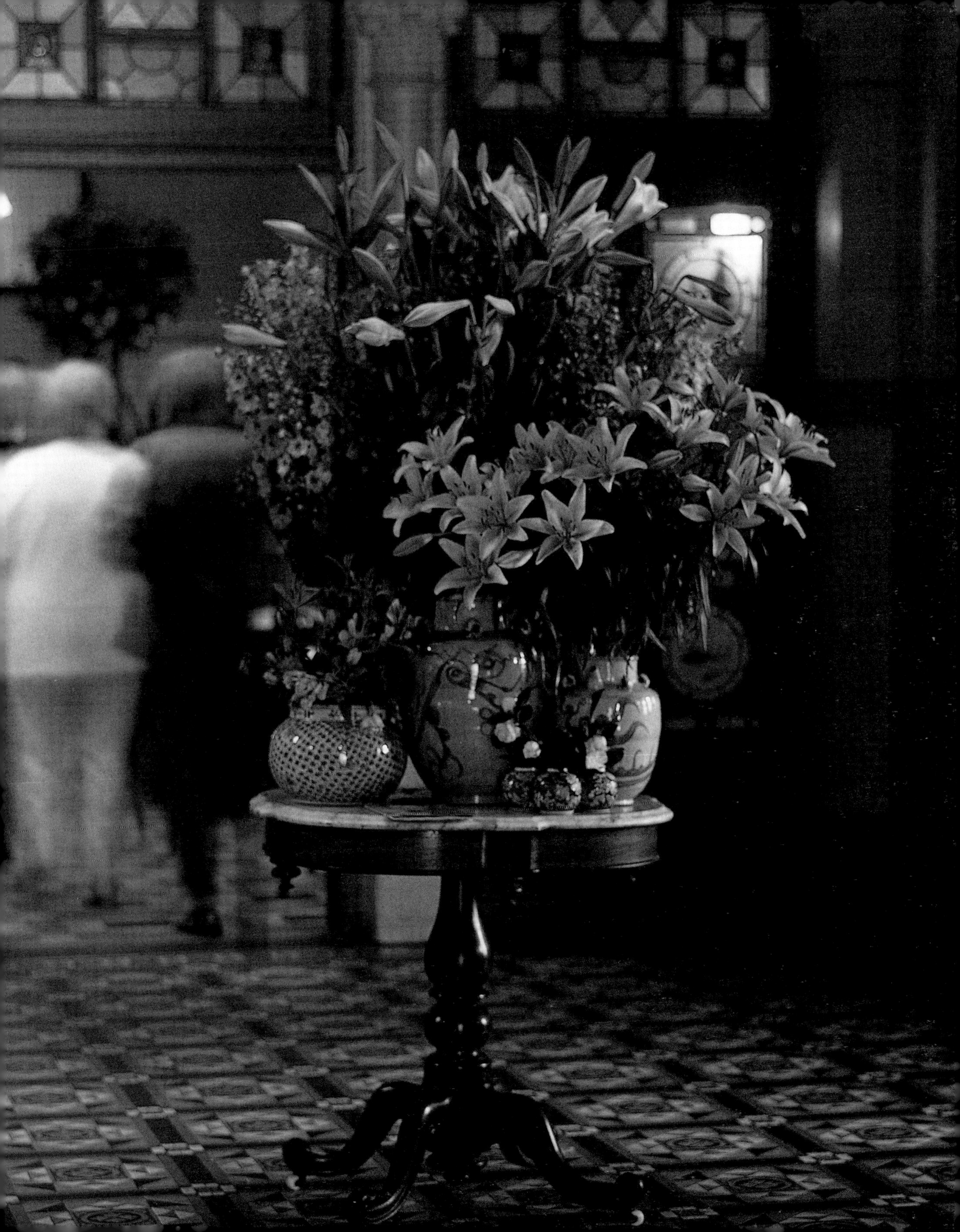

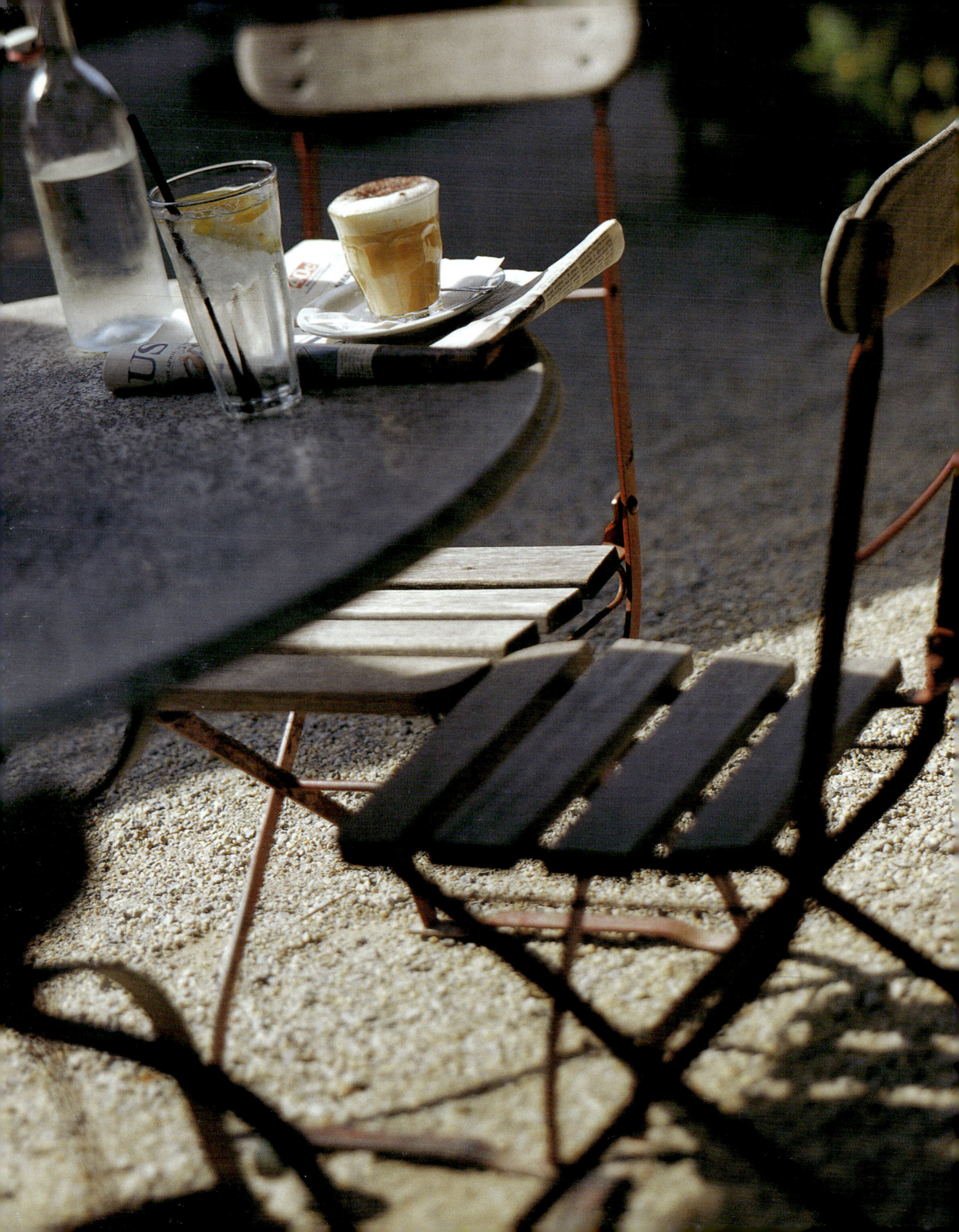

Soho lemonade

Peter Russell Clarke, Soho, Drysdale

Place 1 cup of water, 2 cups of sugar, a pinch of salt and the rind of 2 lemons (cut into strips) into a non-reactive pan. Heat until the sugar has dissolved. Take off the heat and add 1$^1/_2$ cups of lemon juice. Strain and add more lemon juice to make up to 750 ml. Bottle in an airtight container and store in the fridge. To make lemonade, mix 2 tablespoons of cordial with soda water to taste.

Queenscliff, the town, is the kind of romantically stunning and elegant place that seduces you into using old-fashioned words like motoring. Queenscliff, the hotel, right on the sea-front strip of Gellibrand Street, is the kind of place that seduces you full stop. It's a fairytale building of ornate charm and imposing grandeur. Grand but on a human scale. Victorian to the tips of its fine iron lacework, but still incredibly attractive to the modern diner.

Lunch service in the courtyard bistro at Mietta's Queenscliff Hotel officially starts winding up at 2.30 pm. We arrived at 2.20 without a booking, and although we were initially told that we would have to skip entrees we not only managed to squeeze one in (due, in no small part, to my ineffable charm and winning, puppy-dog smile), but also went on to have a relaxed, well-paced meal, without a hint of impatient table-setting indicating 'this is the end of my shift, you know'.

There's a culture of service here that is impeccable: attentive, polite, informative, fast, efficient. A good match for the setting, really: tiled floors, soft light from the conservatory, rustic and sometimes idiosyncratic paintings, the odd touch here and there of old colonial artefacts.

The Queenscliff was built in 1887 for Martha Nugent and Joseph Goslin, and is the youngest of the three grand hotels that still operate grandly in the town. At the time, it was considered that it offered the most luxurious accommodation of all.

The hotel was bought in a thoroughly subdued state (lots of fake panelling and mission brown paintwork) in 1978 by Mietta O'Donnell and Tony Knox, who were then successfully running the now-defunct Mietta's restaurant in Melbourne. Mietta O'Donnell is no longer directly involved — the place is owned and run by her sister, Patricia, who bought the hotel from the family some years ago — but her name is still attached, for history's sake.

There is a fine and sumptuous dining room here, offering a prix fixe menu. Chef Xavier Robinson fits his ingredients to the sumptuousness of the surroundings, but retains an awareness of modern Australian bistro leanings: blue swimmer crab bisque is served with olive and saffron mayonnaise, roast pheasant wrapped in puff pastry comes with parsnip chips and a pear and quince sauce. Desserts include such simple but mouth-watering fare as brandy snaps, stuffed with ricotta mousse on a coffee anglaise.

The food in the more accessible bistro is lighter, easier: ox tongue with mustard, fettuccine with squid and chilli, that kind of thing. I'm glad we charmed our way into a quick shared entree here, because it summed up the attitude of the place. A pile of spanking fresh, huge cold prawns came resting on a jumble of leaves — some frizzy, some succulent — dressed with a sweet and fragrant mango and basil mayonnaisey dressing. Clean, clear flavours, perfect for summer lunch. They know their customer.

The wine list here leans heavily towards the output of Geelong and the Bellarine and Mornington Peninsulas ('The Wines of Our Region'), with some older vintages being offered at excellent prices.

There's also a shop and bar that serves everything snacky from espresso with biscotti and vin santo to a warm beef sandwich, with pizza, salad and Middle Eastern dried fruit salad in between. On summer evenings in the herb garden, a set barbecue menu pulls in the punters in droves, while the popular winemakers' dinners and stand-up comedy evenings with Judith Lucy (casserole, chocolate cake and show for less than forty bucks) are becoming perennial favourites.

Any place that can keep doing all that, day in, day out, and still do it with a relaxed smile deserves huge respect.

The Ozone Hotel

The Ozone — just up the street from Mietta's Queenscliff and similar in scale although a little grander in architecture — has been in constant use as a hotel since it was built in 1881. It was originally called Baillieu House after its owner, James Baillieu, who had arrived in Victoria in 1853 (the current name honours the *Ozone*, one of the steamers that brought customers across the bay from Melbourne). And yes, James was one of those Baillieus — not only one of them, but the first of them.

George Baillieu, one of James' eleven sons, ran the place for the first three decades, and it's not too fanciful to assume that it was here, one sultry summer's night, that George's daughter, Merlyn, first danced with the man she would later marry and start a dynasty with: Sidney Myer.

The current owner of the hotel, Darryl Davidson, took over in 1980 (going on to buy the Vue Grand in 1983) and, like the O'Donnells down the road, inherited a building that was but a shadow of its former self — a fairly ordinary public bar had become the centre of attention, and the grand ballroom was in thorough need of some tender affection. The long, slow, ongoing process of renovation, however, has seen much of the glory return: the bar is no longer open to the public (there's a much more genteel sense of sophistication about it now), and the grand ballroom is once again very grand.

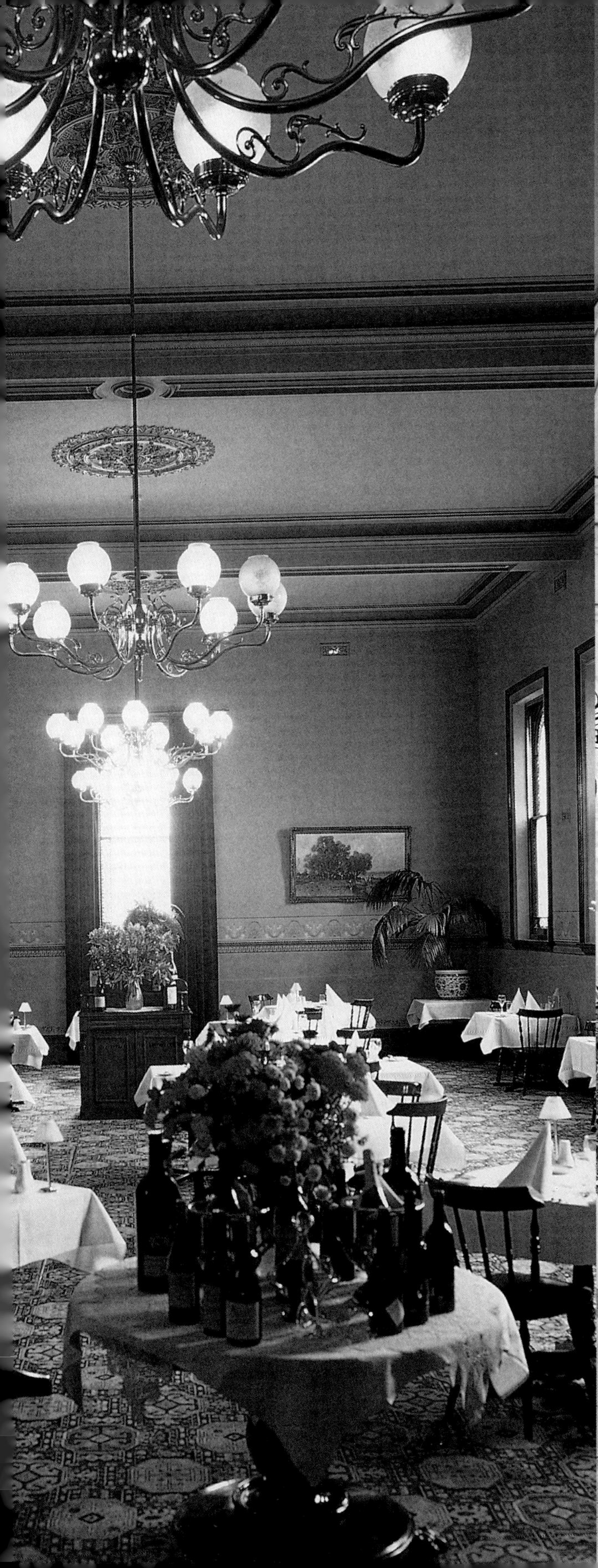

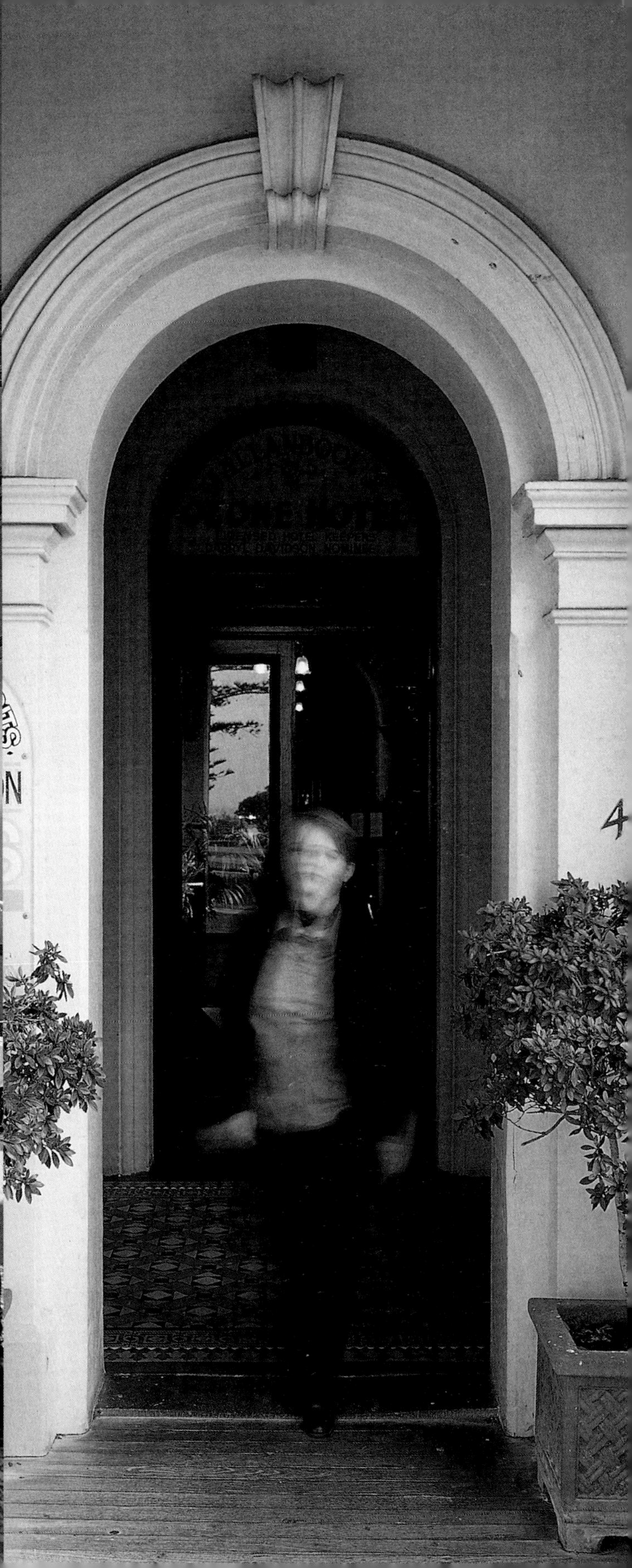

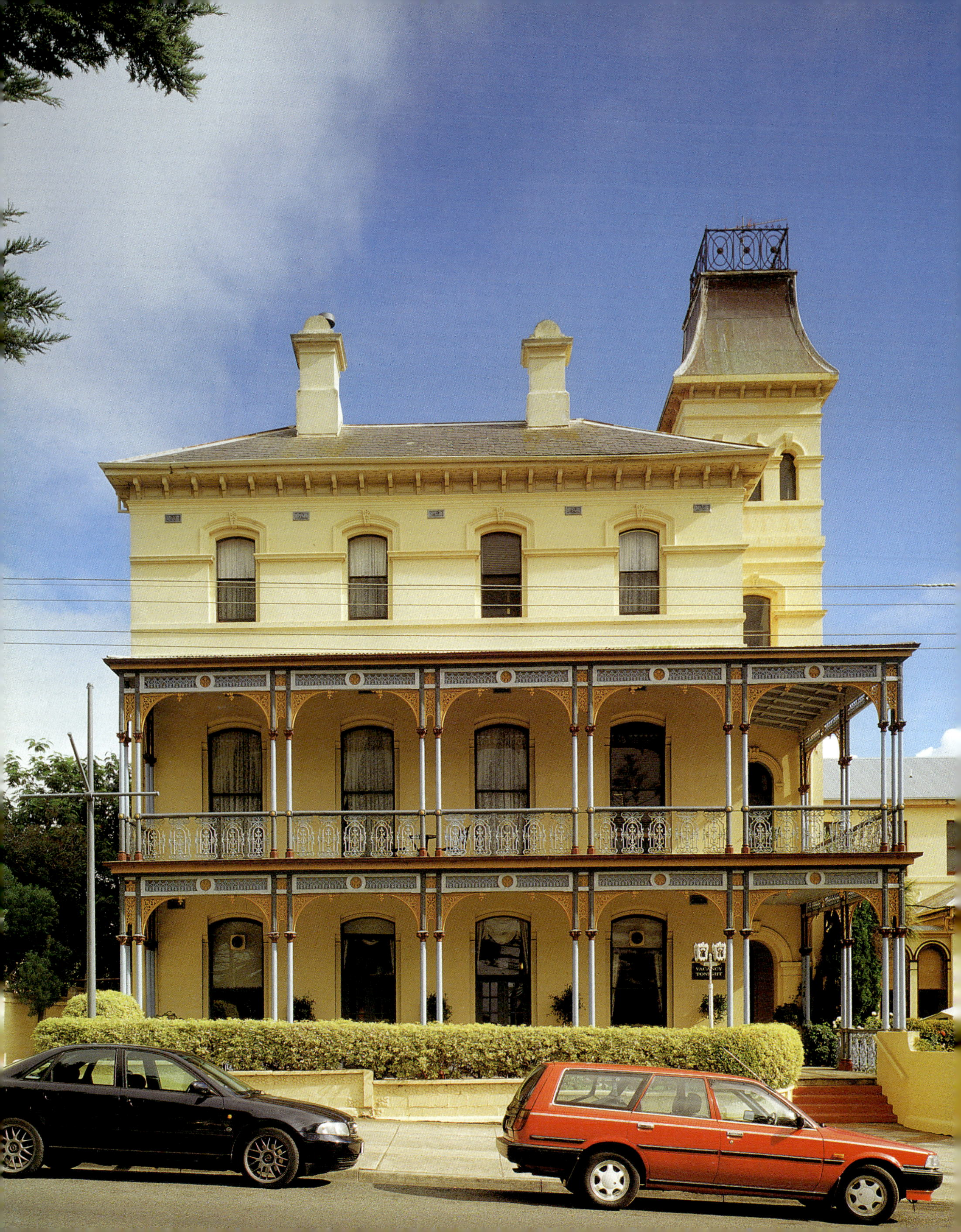

There's a terribly calm atmosphere here in the Ozone's Boat Bar Restaurant. Slightly fading images of the region's maritime past stare down at you from the soft burgundy-coloured walls. As much as possible is made of the history crowding every corner here, just as it is (and just as it should be) at all three of the grand hotels. A conservatory glows green and sedate behind glass windows at one end. Guests chatter and tinkle. A clock ticks warmly on the mantelpiece.

The food that is served up by chef Greg Heath, however, is anything but old-fashioned. Greg's background includes a stint at Piero's in Melbourne's casino, and this city-savvy is reflected in the choice of some ingredients.

Ocean trout, for example, comes as a carpaccio, dressed with a glowing orange emulsion of citrus and soy, brightened even further by a whisper of chilli. And lamb rump comes marinated in harissa (a piquant Middle Eastern paste of hot peppers), roasted and sat atop a plump zucchini and olive frittata with capsicum and a moderately sticky mint-flavoured jus.

But the highlight for me is a dessert: a single poached Corella pear, perched on a mound of mascarpone, surrounded by a moat of orange caramel sauce. The finishing touch is a garnish — not the obligatory mint sprig or half-a-white-strawberry, but an exquisite, delicate orange flower, its petals the colour of mandarin mousse.

Wherever possible, Greg Heath will use local produce: meat is supplied by Henry Penny, one of Geelong's well-established butchers; cheeses on the platter include at least two from Mount Emu Creek; and ice-creams — with such unusual flavours as basil, and lavender — are made by Phil Bitton, again in Geelong (he trades under the name 'Like Heaven', as in Phil's Like Heaven … geddit?). And on the hotel's award-winning wine list, local wines are prominently displayed.

The Ozone is well placed to continue down this track, because although local is not always cheapest, the hotel's large proportion of corporate clients are often happy to pay that little bit extra. It's neither the first nor the last time you will read this sentiment expressed in this book, but you get what you pay for.

The Vue Grand

The Vue Grand is the biggest of the old Queenscliff hotels, but with only thirty-two rooms is still not overly large. It also feels to me — and this probably has as much to do with its size as anything — closest in atmosphere to the original era (how I would know, of course, is anybody's guess). Although the exterior of the building lacks some of the ornate Victorian frippery of the Ozone or Mietta's, internally it is by far the most opulent and lavish of them all.

Wandering through the hotel with the general manager, I was told that the high-ceilinged breakfast room here used to be inhabited by the kitchens when the hotel had over 100 rooms. And for a split-second, hot urgent images of white-toqued chefs and armies of terrified kitchen hands flashed like ghosts through my mind's eye. Then again, I had just finished my eighth short macchiato of the day, so such hallucinations are not all that surprising.

The Vue Grand has had a huge past. It opened in 1881, the same year as work commenced on the Ozone. Its large scale — and particularly its large ballroom and resident band — made it one of the most popular places among the visiting socialites. In October 1927 it drew even larger crowds when fire took hold and destroyed a third of the hotel. And in 1983 it was — unlike the other two places profiled here — totally renovated and restored, with extensive conference, gym, pool and recreational facilities (stop me, I sound like a brochure).

Left • The Ozone.

Much of the Vue Grand's success lies in the long-standing relationship and influence of the general manager, Vladimir Hradil, and executive chef, Stephane le Grand. Czech-born and Hilton-trained Hradil has been here since the hotel's refurbishment. Le Grand, whose experience includes time at a three-Michelin-starred Parisian restaurant, Amboisy, and working for two of Melbourne's top French chefs, Jacques Reymond and Philippe Mouchel, has been in the kitchens here for six years — a long time in the hotel game.

The cooking at the Vue Grand is by far the most adventurous and worked of the three hotels. For most of the time, le Grand offers a slightly unorthodox but fairly straightforward à la carte menu: roast chicken salad with warrigal greens and sherry vinegar; saffron fettuccine with salmon and sundried tomato coulis; peppered pork with enoki mushrooms, bok choy and beetroot jus — that kind of thing.

But for Saturday dinner in the Grand dining room, chef goes to town, offering a fixed-price menu of sometimes staggering lavishness and complexity. Try a pyramid of panfried prawns marinated in fenugreek served with deep fried celery with an apple balsamic and macadamia oil vinaigrette. Or kangaroo fillet marinated in cardamom surrounded by a cucumber confit, served with ginger jus. Phew.

The alert reader will by now have picked up an undertone of bush-food savvy in here, and the alert reader would be right: warrigal greens, lemon balm, quandong all appear. (The alert reader will also have detected a touch of pomposity, too, and again, the alert reader would be right: for example, describing corn as 'maize kernels', whilst correct, is just silly; and 'Creme de Chiboust of Golden Apple resting on a midori gelee [sic]' is positively Pythonesque.)

What interests me more is an active, intelligent and proud use of local produce. Screaming Seeds spice mixes are used as marinades (dukkah in the veal terrine, Kashmiri Krush on the beef); and quail is served with shallots and a Scotchmans Hill pinot noir sauce. Such detail says a lot to me: it tells me not only that the chef is aware of the quality of locally produced food and wine, but that he is proud to name the supplier of that produce — ensuring supply and consistency to the diner. It's a practical thing, as much as a philosophical one.

Having said that though, what le Grand does behind the scenes here is perhaps his most valuable and long-lasting contribution to local gastronomy. Every chef and apprentice in his kitchen is local — from the Bellarine Peninsula or Geelong. Everyone is trained from day one. Everyone is taught everything, from bread making to the exceptionally fine and complicated presentation skills that le Grand's grander dishes require.

And some of those who have passed through le Grand's kitchen are beginning to spread the reputation of Queenscliff's cooks elsewhere. A new take on the concept of promoting regional food?

10 eccentric places to stay along the great ocean road

King Parrot, Pennyroyal

Horden Vale House, Aire Valley

Allenvale Cottages, Lorne

Pennyroyal Raspberry Farm, Pennyroyal

Elliminook, Birregurra

Gobles Millhouse, Port Fairy

Bush to Beach, Aireys Inlet

Cape Otway Cottages, Cape Otway

New Beginnings, Fairhaven

Wollaston, Warrnambool

VUE GRAND HOTEL

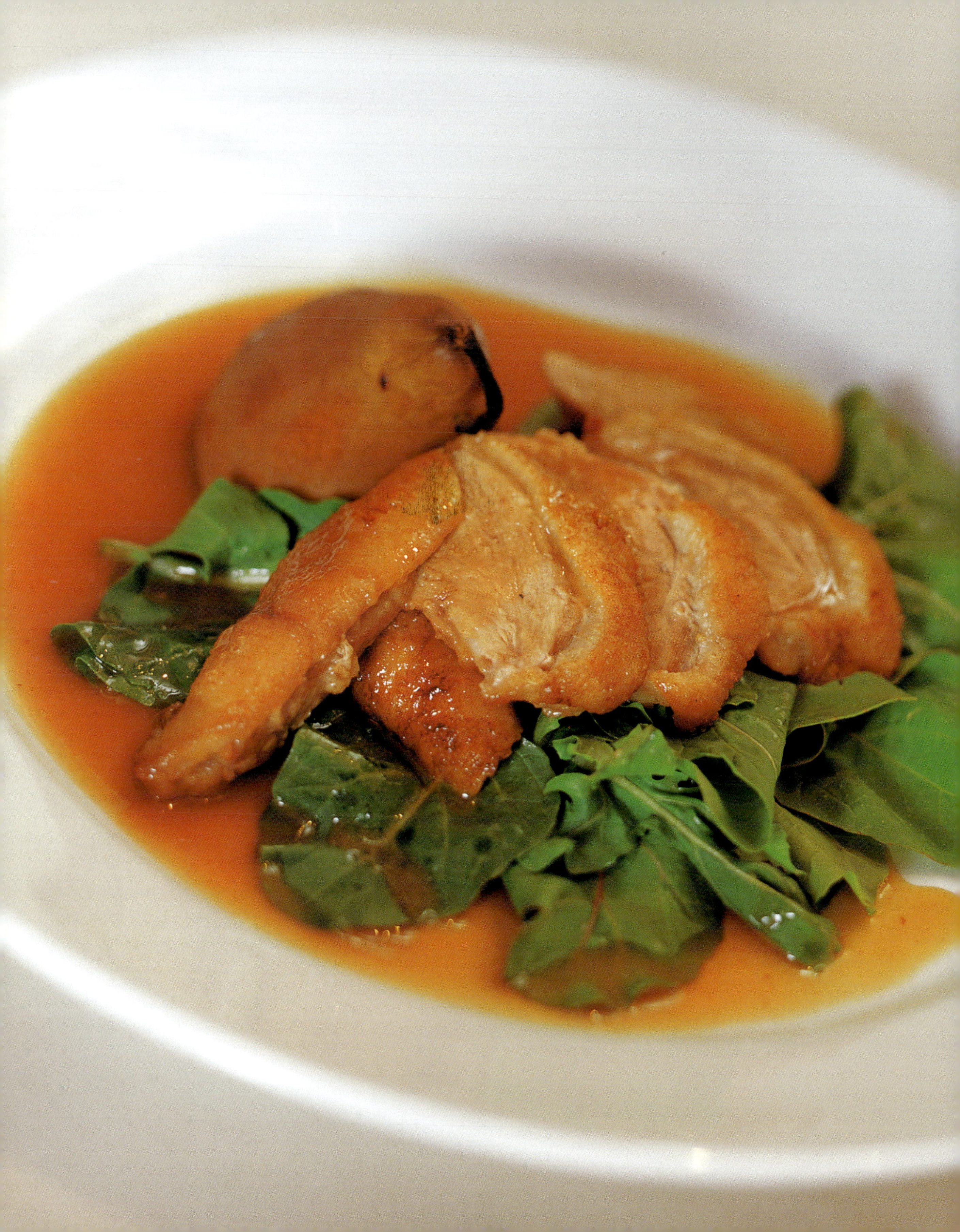

New Year's Eve at the Turn of the Century

Vine-ripened Tomato Consommé
with Quenelles of Eel

Gâteau of King Crab with Scallops

Duck with Aperol, Pear
and Wild Rocket

Artichoke and Potato Galette

Spinach with Garlic

Passionfruit Brûlée Tart with
Ginger Cream, Warm Compote of Berries
and a Poppyseed Wafer

Vine-ripened Tomato Consomme with Quenelles of Eel

Tousson, Geelong

Serves 6

Consomme

3 French shallots, finely chopped

olive oil

3 cloves garlic, finely sliced

1 tsp Maldon sea salt

1 tsp sugar

1 tsp chopped basil, tarragon & chervil

1 kg vine-ripened tomatoes coarsely chopped

1 litre light chicken stock

4 egg whites

6 black peppercorns

6 coriander seeds

Quenelles

200 g smoked eel

2 egg whites

100 ml cream (35% fat)

Garnish

100 g tomato concasse

40 g soaked dried porcini mushrooms or sliced small 'slippery jack' mushrooms

1 tsp julienne of basil

In a large saucepan, sweat the shallots in the olive oil until they just begin to colour. Add the garlic, salt and sugar, chopped herbs and half of the tomatoes. Cook on a gentle heat for about 15 minutes.

Add the chicken stock and bring to the boil, then skim and simmer for 10 minutes. Pass through a fine strainer. Cool the liquid on ice.

Liquidise the remaining tomatoes, egg whites, peppercorns and coriander seeds. Whisk into the cooled tomato stock. To clarify, bring slowly to the boil and simmer for about 20 minutes until the liquid becomes clear and carefully strain through muslin and cool quickly. Cool all ingredients.

Puree eel with egg whites, add cream and process quickly. Season. Pass through a fine mouli and form into quenelles. Place on non-stick paper.

Place the quenelles on the paper in a shallow saucepan. Pour on hot consomme and poach for about 5 minutes until cooked. Remove.

To assemble, bring the consomme to the boil. In a separate pan reheat a little consomme, spoon into warm soup bowls, quickly blanch the mushrooms and add to the soup bowls. Divide the tomato concasse and julienne of basil between the bowls and ladle the consomme over.

Gâteau of King Crab with Scallops

Vue Grand, Queenscliff

Serves 4

Gâteau

60 g carrots

60 g leeks

60 g celery

60 g turnips

20 g shallots

250 g scallops, lightly poached

10 slices of Tasmanian smoked salmon

250 g king crab meat

Mayonnaise

4 egg yolks

1 small spoon of mustard

2 cups olive oil

1 cup of vegetable oil

20 g flat parsley

1 tsp tandoori paste

30 ml sherry vinegar

salt and pepper

Garnishes

watercress

1 cup coconut milk

1 cucumber

some fresh coconut, grated

Dice the vegetables. Blanch the carrots, 10 g of leeks, celery, turnips and shallots. Combine.

Prepare the mayonnaise by combining the egg yolks, mustard and remaining leeks until whipped then gradually drop the oil in. Add the tandoori paste, sherry vinegar, salt and pepper, and stir in the chopped parsley.

Mix the mayonnaise, the small dice of vegetables, king crab and half of the scallops together with the coconut milk. Put a slice of smoked salmon in the mould and then fill with the mix. Place the watercress on the plate, surround these with the coconut milk, cucumber and grated coconut.

Press the mix out of the mould, then add 2-3 scallops on the top of the mould.

Duck with Aperol, Pear and Wild Rocket

Sempre Cafe, Geelong

Serves 6

2 kg duck bones

1 carrot

1 onion

2 sticks celery

3 litres water

300 ml Aperol (a syrup made from bitter orange and rhubarb, available at good liquor merchants)

6 duck breasts

200 ml olive oil

salt

6 Corella (Red Sensation) pears

250 g wild rocket

Place the duck bones along with vegetables in oven for about 25 minutes until slightly brown. Put into a large pot, add cold water. Bring to the boil. Simmer for 4 hours, skimming the surface regularly to remove impurities.

Continue adding small amounts of water to sustain level. Strain. Dispose of bones and vegetables. Place stock in pot and reduce by two-thirds.

Add Aperol (off the heat). Place back on flame and reduce by half. (This sauce can be made up to several days prior to requiring).

To roast breast, oil slightly and rub salt liberally into skin. Place skin up on baking tray and roast for 15-20 minutes in hot oven.

Place pears on tray in oven 5 minutes prior to the completion of the duck. Remove duck from oven and allow to rest. On a large, warm plate, place washed rocket leaves in a mound. Carve breast in half and place on top. Pour hot sauce over duck and allow to flood plate. Garnish with whole roasted pear.

Artichoke and Potato Galette

Sunnybrae Country Restaurant, Birregurra

Serves 6

6 medium artichokes cooked in salted water to which the juice of 3 lemons has been added
200 g cooked Desiree potatoes
salt and pepper

Mash artichokes and potatoes together, season and form into galettes with a scone cutter. Place on an oiled baking tray and cook in a medium oven until the bases are crisp.

Spinach with Garlic

Marks Restaurant, Lorne

Serves 6

6 cloves garlic
sea salt and pepper
60 g butter
500 g spinach leaves
touch of olive oil

Crush garlic with some sea salt and pepper. Set aside. Wash spinach and quickly blanch in salted water. Saute with a touch of olive oil, butter and garlic. Season to taste.

Passionfruit Brûlée Tart with Ginger Cream, Warm Compote of Berries and a Poppyseed Wafer

Marine Cafe, Lorne

Serves 12

Pastry

250 g butter
200 g icing sugar
500 g flour
½ tsp vanilla extract
2 eggs, beaten
2 egg yolks, beaten

Process butter, icing sugar, flour in a food processor until it resembles wet breadcrumbs. Spread out on a workbench and drizzle with beaten eggs so they are evenly spread. Bring together into a ball. Do not overwork. Wrap in plastic and rest for at least 1 hour in a cool spot.

Roll out into a sheet between 2 pieces of 'Go-Between' a little larger than the flan (remember the depth). Rest for at least 1 hour. Keep the excess pastry for patching later.

Blind bake at 140°C. When cooked, seal with a mix of egg whites and a little water.

Filling

300 ml cream
9 eggs
350 g castor sugar
350 ml seedless passionfruit juice

Lightly whip the cream, then mix thoroughly with the eggs, sugar, and the passionfruit juice.

Pour into warm cooked tart shell. Bake at 120°C for about 35 minutes.

Poppyseed Wafer

75 g butter
25 g honey
75 g sugar
25 g poppyseeds
125 g sesame seeds
25 g milk

Melt butter and honey. Add sugar, stir in, add seeds. Stir in and add cold milk. Stir. Rest till thick. Paste onto non-stick paper. Bake at 190°C till golden. Remove and shape.

Ginger Cream

200 ml cream
1 tsp powdered ginger
1 tsp sugar

Whisk together, cover and chill.

Berry Compote

50 g sugar
water
100 g blueberries
100 g raspberries

Cook sugar and water to a syrup, adding berry juices. Add berries and set aside.

Serve the tart with the berry compote, ginger cream and the wafer.

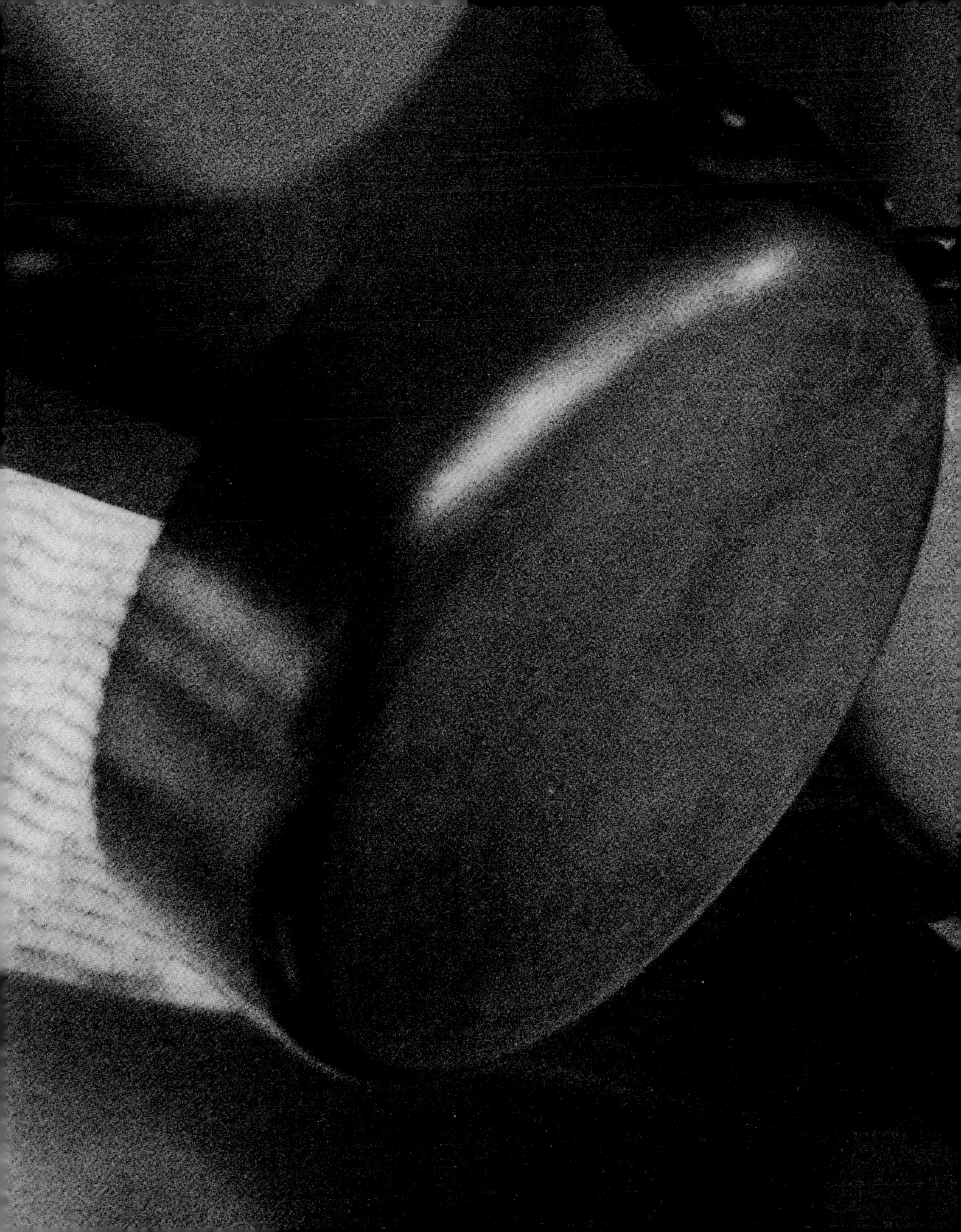

kitchens and cooks

Position, position, position. If it's the golden rule of real estate and restaurants, then both the houses and the eateries along the Great Ocean Road have one of the best natural advantages in the world. From the waterfront in Geelong to the tree-lined streets of Port Fairy, you'll find some of Victoria's most beautifully positioned restaurants.

Fishermen's Pier and Le Parisien, Geelong's highest-profile, established nosh-houses, share their view of the increasingly smart waterfront precinct. The diner at either place stares out at shimmering blue water, the You Yangs rising from the horizon across the bay, gently tinkling fishing boats, and the odd lone seagull, whilst tucking into a glass of local chardonnay and fish of the day, simply prepared.

In Lorne, restaurants such as Kosta's and Mark's jostle for your attention along Mountjoy Parade, opening out to the bustling street during summer, full to bursting with holiday makers nursing hangovers behind sunglasses, and cradling caffe lattes. The shriek of kids drifts up from the beach, a hop, skip and a jump away.

At Apollo Bay, the mist can roll in across the beach, turning this wide sweep of normally stunning country into one of the most magical places on earth — perfect when viewed with glass of shiraz in hand at sea level at the Sea Grape Wine Bar, or from above, through fine grey gum trees at Chris's Beacon Point up in the hills.

And at Port Fairy, the restaurants open out to Norfolk-pine-lined Georgian streets, perambulating visitors and antique hunters — not to mention the odd young feller determined to enjoy as much of the town's thoroughly Irish-influenced hospitality as possible.

But enough of the hype. All these picturesque panoramas would mean diddly-squat if the food on your plate wasn't able to match the view. In many cases, thankfully, it is: there is little doubt that there is better eating to be had along the Great Ocean Road now than ever before.

Food down here is in a constant state of flux. It changes as the tastes of the consumer change. Geelong food writer Gail Thomas is flabbergasted at how this has happened. 'It's amazing when you talk to the young,' she says. 'They have no recollection of the old food here — no memories of taking your pot up to the Chinese take-away. Now the children of the older generation are coming through and they are embracing cafe life.'

And the more these sophisticated diners flow down the Road, the more places open or change their menus to suit. Espresso machines are now commonplace, but this is a surprisingly recent phenomenon. The Greek influence, so strong in Lorne and Apollo Bay, has made itself felt in small doses in other places. Mediterranean is big — not surprisingly, when you're beside the sea.

But while more and more Acland Street-clone bistros crop up incongruously in seafront strips otherwise dominated by fish-and-chip shops and pubs — all catering to a perceived demand — there is also a strong yearning among many visitors for the more humble, easy, less refined eating experience. As one friend in the restaurant trade said to me: 'I go on holiday to the Great Ocean Road to get away from posh restaurants.'

I'd be lying if I said that every restaurant, cafe and bistro along the Great Ocean Road from Queenscliff to Portland lives up either to the view or even to the laziest food-lover's expectations. Greasy chips, soggy pasta, grated carrot garnishes and terrible service are, unfortunately, all too commonly encountered. But the good places I've profiled in this chapter more than make up for the bad ones: they are reason in themselves to travel the Road.

Above • Flaming prawns at Fishermen's Pier, Geelong.

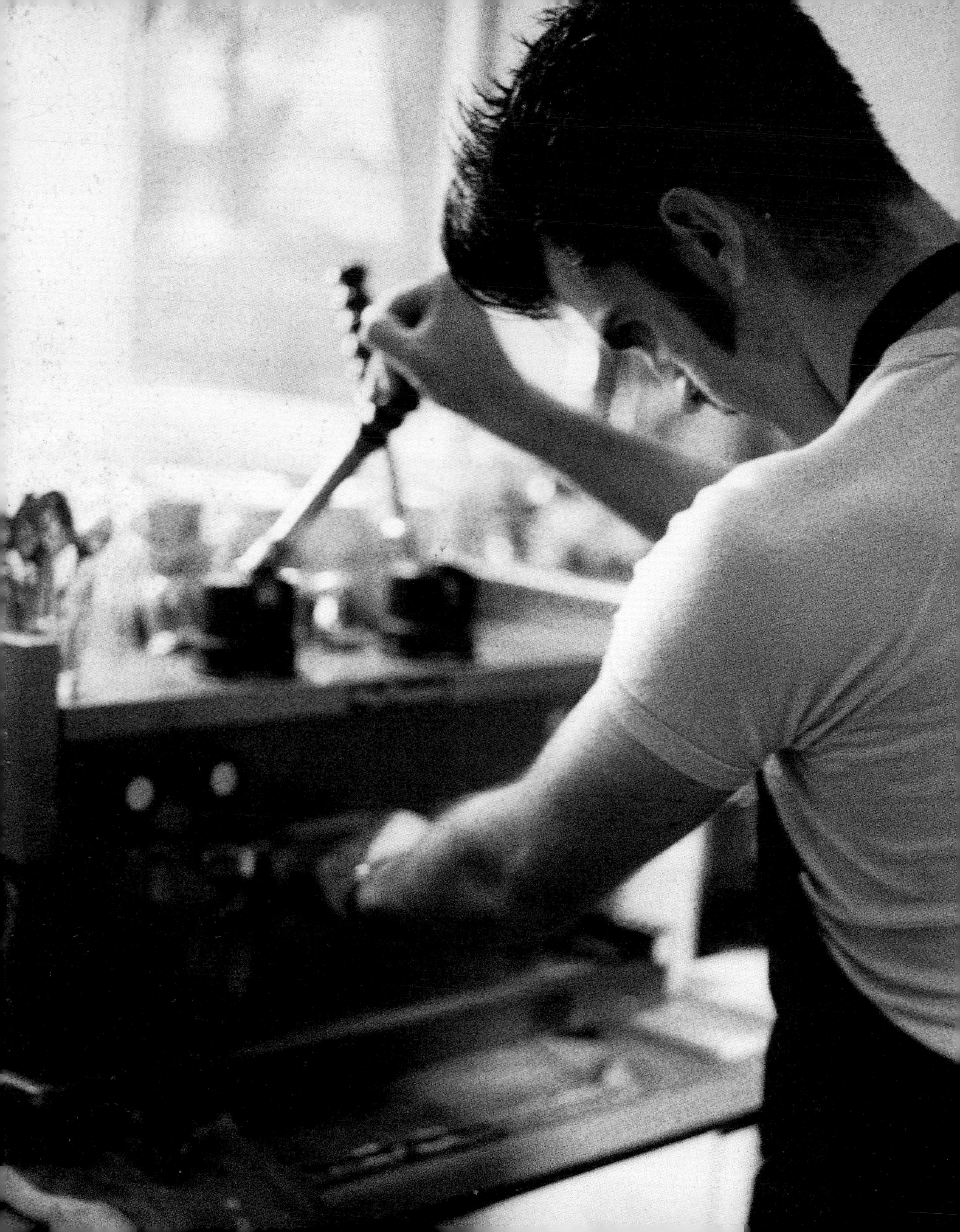

Geelong: Sempre

For me, the most exciting restaurant in Geelong is one of its smallest and also one of its newest. The barely one-year-old Sempre, squeezed snugly into a narrow shop on Little Malop Street right in the centre of town, describes itself as a 'caffe e paninoteca', and is modelled fairly and squarely on the small, drop-dead-groovy Melbourne Italian bistros, Caffe e Cucina and Il Bacaro.

This is far from surprising when you consider the background of the owners/chefs. Chris Taranto, Andrew Koch and Mary de Leo have all been through the Cucina mill. But this is no Cucina-clone. All three of the young people behind Sempre are originally Geelong kids: work experience includes stints at two of Geelong's well-established dining rooms, the Empire Grill and Giussepe's.

So the decision to open Sempre was motivated less by a desire to copy big-city-chic, and more by a desire to serve good, accessible food in a modern setting to a new wave of Geelong diners who had become perhaps a touch too familiar with the same old menus and spaces.

And this is the important point. Since it opened in a relatively low-key kind of way in 1998, Sempre has been swamped by hungry Geelong diners, keen as mostarda to get some of Koch and de Leo's food into them. Not to mention the Italian wines on offer now that Taranto has got himself a licence (it is also BYO and attracts a heavy following from among the local wine fraternity).

This great response has come as a bit of a surprise to Sempre's owners. For a start, the place does not look like a conventional Geelong restaurant. The colour scheme is deep purple, glowing blue tiles, bold Campari posters, and Alessi pepper grinders. Funky, loungey Hammond music ripples from the speakers. But it feels right. It feels like it's been here for much longer than it has.

10 places that serve seriously good coffee

Cafe Felix, Geelong

Empire Grill, Geelong

Figaro's Deli and Cafe, Geelong

Guiseppe's Cafe, Geelong

Kosta's, Lorne

Moons Cafe, Lorne

One 5 Three, Apollo Bay

Mietta's Queenscliff Hotel, Queenscliff

Sempre, Geelong

The Bay Leaf Cafe, Apollo Bay

Left • Chris Taranto, at Sempre, Geelong.

The menu features many of the classics, such as bruschetta, zinging-fresh calamari fritti, pollo con prosciutto (ham-topped chook breast on pea puree with lemon butter) and tortellini with delicate duck stuffing — not to mention the old faithful, tiramisu. But it also contains some dishes that are fairly unusual even by Melbourne standards (which sounds so patronising, but you know what I mean).

The more adventurous dishes include carpaccio di pesce (wafer-thin slices of raw, cured fish with capers and lemon), a sweet orange risotto (risotto della casa) of caramelised leeks and sweet potato, and the thoroughly addictive dessert called affogato: a scoop of ice-cream served with an espresso which you pour over the ice-cream, and a shot of liqueur of your choice to do likewise with (I prefer Frangelico, but that's just me). There are also deliciously local ingredients such as authentic fennel sausages made by a bloke in the suburbs of Geelong.

Taranto and Koch tell a story of two young kids out on a date (and I took that to mean two people in at least their last year of teenage — which is rich coming from Taranto and Koch, hardly old men themselves). They looked like 'scared little rabbits' when they came in, apparently, but by the time they left they'd had a whale of a time, and tried things that amazed the owners — even the gorgonzola ice-cream and fresh apple that Sempre serve as an entree (which I have to admit I find daunting). A fair amount of the Italian digestif, Aperol had also been consumed — an acquired taste for even the most seasoned bistro-goer.

Something new is being forged by the people at Sempre and they deserve all the support they can get.

Geelong: Wholefoods

Just around the corner from Sempre is Wholefoods Cafe, a place with just as much passion but a quite different feel to it. Not to be confused with Geelong's other Whole Foods, the organic co-operative, the Wholefoods Cafe and Gallery was set up in this spot in 1990 by John and Jan Farnan, ex-teacher and librarian respectively, but had been going for a good few years before that at another location.

The couple were driven by a love of good food and a scarcity of the same in Geelong at the time. From the beginning, organic produce and organic flour were the basis for the cooking and breadmaking here. Today's menu includes such wholesome offerings as calzone, a sourdough pastry pocket filled with antipasto ingredients and pecorino cheese; and dahl, zucchini and sweetcorn soup.

John is one of the John Downes (Natural Tucker) school of sourdough baking, and his breads are excellent, benefiting from being made using a sixteen-year-old culture. In more recent times, it has become easier to source locally-produced stuff, too, so this has become a minor feature.

'There are the beginnings of a network,' says John. 'I grow herbs and we've got close to sixty chooks, so we're well supplied with eggs. We get a few local carrots and potatoes, there's a lady who grows decorative lettuces, a couple of lemon trees and some goats' ricotta we get from a backyarder who comes in with his tubs.'

But for his wines, John Farnan casts his net wider. He's decided to run with organic wines, and has unearthed some beauties — especially the range from Glenara in the Adelaide Hills. Having said that, though, his big coup was discovering that Prince Albert, situated just down the road outside Geelong, is an organically-run vineyard.

It fits the place's philosophy perfectly.

Far left • Chef/owners of Sempre Chris Taranto and Andrew Koch.
Left • At the bar at Sempre.
Right • John Farnan, of Wholefoods Cafe and Gallery, Geelong.

Geelong: POP

Lindsay Powell has been running the successful Cafe Botticelli in Pakington Street, Geelong, for nine years. He has succeeded because he has been flexible: if people want the posh dinner, Botticelli can provide. If all they want is coffee and cake then that's fine, too.

Now he is taking on the fast-food giants with a hole-in-the-wall operation (literally) one door down from Botticelli. Called Pop Food Express, it offers trays of take-away food ranging from better-than-average pizza slices to mouth-wateringly huge rafts of char-grilled pide bread stuffed to the gills with Moroccan-spiced vegetables, harissa and yoghurt; and rolls encasing Angel Cardoso's chorizos. Given a choice between an overly salty burger with fries and that lot, I know which I'd choose.

You can't miss Pop: it distinguishes itself by its huge glowing red balls hanging outside. It opens for lunch and closes when the food runs out.

Dry Scallops

When buying scallops look for the small firm ones. They are slightly brown and if they look a little muddy this is good. The big white fluffy ones have been soaked in water. They can absorb their whole weight in water, so you will be paying $20 a kilo for water. Always ask for 'dry' scallops.

Queenscliff: Harry's

Some of my most memorable nosh-ups have been in seafront restaurants. Tucking into black-pepper wok-fried crab by the beach in Penang; sipping sparkling wine at my wedding reception looking at the sun setting over the sands of St Kilda; devouring prawns and the local bone-dry sherry in Sanlucar de Barrameda in southern Spain; polishing off a paella in the port of Cadaques in northern Spain (oops, sorry, there I go, drifting off again...). One of the best feeds I had researching this book was also within a pebble's throw of the beach — at Harry's, slap-bang in the middle of Princess Park on the foreshore in Queenscliff.

At first glance, the casual observer might dismiss this small place as nothing more than a fish and chip shop. It certainly looks like one — pretty bare, a counter and blue walls, lots of flaking white paint, a glary glass-walled dining room out back, fairly brusque service and a radio tuned to PBS, a Melbourne alternative station, blaring out obscure Motown.

But the casual observer would be sadly mistaken. The small, ever-changing hand-written blackboard menu here is one of the Road's most interesting — not to mention one of its most up-to-date. And the chef here knows fish better than almost anyone else around.

Michael Barrett came to Australia from Ireland when he was thirteen. He trained in the kitchens of various top Sydney hotels, and originally came to Melbourne to help set up another posh hotel. He found himself cooking for Chris Talihmanidis in 1984, however, and ended up staying, later becoming head chef at the Queenscliff Hotel before taking over this beach-front position ten years ago.

From the beginning, Barrett has tried to weave various outside influences through the cooking of top-quality seafood (most of which he gets, by the way, from White Fisheries in St Leonards). So on the day I went the menu listed universally appealing standards such as smoked salmon on corn fritters with lemon mayo; yabbies with citrus and watercress salad; and mussels with butter, spring onion and white wine.

But it also listed 'wing' of schnapper in a miso broth (a heartily graphic and deep-tasting dish not for the squeamish: lots of bones and tails and fins but terrific flavour) and marlin with shiitake mushrooms and Chinese vegies in miso broth. Oh, and seafood isn't offered exclusively: again, two standouts from the menu the day I went included beef tap tap (a rich and wild curry); and braised duck leg with prosciutto, tarragon and grilled polenta.

But seafood is the main event — and ironically, Harry's stands apart from many other local restaurants in this respect. 'Surprisingly few people are focussing on seafood down here,' says Barrett. 'A lot of that has to do with supply. We still get whiting, schnapper, mussels, squid, but the supply is dwindling. There are not as many commercial fishermen as there used to be; not many of the young fellers are coming into it.' Still enough to keep him happy though.

Barrett does most of the cooking himself in fairly cramped conditions. Consequently, he is only open for dinner and Saturday lunch through the summer. But when he is open he's popular. Harry's is also still, thankfully, BYO. The perfect place, then, to take the spoils of a hard day's cellar-door raiding amongst the Geelong and Bellarine wineries.

The food is not terribly 'refined', and certainly not complicated at Harry's, but that's its strength: it has a stamp of originality and personality so often lacking in many other restaurants in the region.

Above • Kosta and Pam Talihmanidis outside their restaurant in Lorne.

Lorne: Kosta's

Oh, to be in Lorne in the summertime ... If you can stand the crowds and the endless multicoloured reflections of the sun from a million wraparound sunnies, then it is a great place to be. Glorious views, good beaches and most important of all of course for this tummy-led tourist, good tucker.

Lorne, you could argue, is the best-served of all the Great Ocean Road towns when it comes to food. As well as the long-standing institutions such as The Arab (where who you are seen eating with is far more important than what you are eating), and The Pier, Lorne residents and visitors have the rather smart, modern city-edged Mark's, the thoroughly Greek-influenced Marine Cafe (run by Phil Talihmanidis, son of Chris — of whom, more later), and the newer Qdos, a gallery-cafe up in the bush behind the town.

But for me, the one restaurant that best sums up the spirit of food and drink in Lorne is Kosta's Taverna, an oasis of bright, light hospitality right on the main drag of Mountjoy Parade.

In many ways, the story of Kosta's (and the Marine, for that matter) is tied intimately to that of Chris's at Beacon Point, profiled next. Indeed, it may make more sense to read that story first before reading this one, although reading them simultaneously would be ideal. That way you would best see the profound influence the Talihmanidis brothers, their partners and offspring have had on the good food culture of this part of the world.

Kosta Talihmanidis arrived in Australia in 1974. He had come out to help his brother Chris at the restaurant Chris had established in the bush overlooking Apollo Bay. The brothers — how shall we put this? — had a parting of ways

(Kosta is the more laid-back, rough-and-ready flip side to Chris's suave, collected charm), and Kosta ended up in Lorne, where Chris had previously run the Marine.

Kosta decided to go out on his own, and opened his Taverna in 1976. At about the same time, he met Pam, now his wife and head chef (with Damian Barnes) of the restaurant. Sitting outside Kosta's at one of the street tables one late summer's morning, Kosta related a story of those early days that summed up how difficult it must have been.

'Lorne was a village then,' he said. 'Open in summer, closed in winter. That didn't really change until about six years ago. When I first started going out with Pam, I was a Greek boy who liked fast cars and beautiful women. All the boys round here liked the footy and getting pissed down the pub. One night we were walking home and got jumped. That's how I got this.'

He points to his slightly crooked nose. Then he points to the front door of the restaurant.

'They also put a fist through that. So the next day I went out and had a new one made, with 'Kosta's Taverna' written in big letters on it. Nobody has touched it since.'

Since the beginning, Kosta and Pam have tried to make their restaurant as welcoming as possible. When they started, they say, there was a snobbish element to the Lorne visitors. But now there is a greater cross-section of families, ethnic groups, and international tourists.

There is certainly a very welcoming sense of style here, from the Miro-like breezy, sketchy murals on the walls to the Dale Hickey-designed sign and logo and the Chris Connell-designed accommodation out the back called the Phoenix Apartments (converted from the local squash courts a couple of years ago).

The menu, as you'd expect, includes such Greek classics as meze, vegetable moussaka and Greek salad, but also trawls a wider part of the Mediterranean (and elsewhere) for inspiration: char-grilled marlin with braised raddichio, olive oil and lemon; porterhouse with tomato chutney, grilled scallops with grapefruit, avocado and poppyseed dressing.

Local ingredients are used, but sparingly: the ciabatta is from Belmont Bakery in Geelong, the beef is from the Western District, the olive oil is from Coonawarra (well it's not that far really, when you think about it), and the vegies, where possible, are local and organic — the vlita, a bushy Greek green leaf vegetable, and the jerusalem artichokes, among other things, are from a tiny vegie patch out the back of the restaurant: 'Organic, too,' says Pam, 'so the kids can eat them.'

Kosta has also been instrumental in a small way in developing one local product in particular: when Robert Manifold was developing his sheeps' milk feta, says Kosta, he was down every week with samples, asking the Greek-born restaurateur if he was getting it right.

So why don't Mount Emu Creek products appear all that often on the menu here? 'They're expensive,' says Kosta. 'And when we do buy any, I just end up eating it all.'

Which doesn't do a lot for promoting local produce, but does a hell of a lot for Kosta's quality of life.

The Rookery Nook Hotel

Let's get one thing straight right away: you don't have to be a surfie to eat or drink at the Rookery Nook Hotel in Wye River. But it helps. No, seriously, this gorgeously situated pub, with its stunning views of pristine white beaches and the deep blue sea beyond, its ample decking and friendly locals, is a great place to eat whether you're a surfie, a townie or just plain hungry.

Chefs Peter Dixon and Kelly Ritchie know that their clientele straddle the social spectrum (so to speak), and cook accordingly. So if you're after something as simple as nachos or spag bol it's there. But if you fancy something a little more adventurous (for pub food) like warm kangaroo salad, then you'll probably find it on special.

The point is that the quality of this pub food is a good two or three notches above the usual: fresh ingredients, well prepared, generously served and well priced.

There are plenty of pubs along the Great Ocean Road — their history is rich with tales of suspicious burnings-down, colourful publicans, grand events and community spirit. I've eaten in many of them, downed the odd cold pot or two in a few others, but I reckon the Rookery Nook — ironically the youngest licensed premises in the region — encapsulates what is best about the easy lifestyle of the Road.

Apollo Bay:
Chris's at Beacon Point

Eating and drinking along the Great Ocean Road reaches a high point at Chris's. Okay, so it's a cheap pun (the restaurant and accommodation are set up in the bush at Beacon Point, with stunning views down to Skenes Creek and Apollo Bay), but it also happens to be true.

Take a simple entree of dips, olives, bread. There is an intensity of flavour in even this simple food that sets the scene for what is to come: the olives, from Greece, are fleshier than usual, tangy; the eggplant dip is ethereally smoky, lusciously textured; the tzatziki has thrilling herbiness; the olive oil is full, fruity, round (and it's Australian); the bread is cakey, generous. Explosions of clear flavour on the tongue.

Other entrees are more complicated; one, a crab salad, has moulded layers of tomato dice, avocado and crab meat remoulade. Main courses, while far from fussy, can be indulgent: chicken fillets glazed with honey, ginger and garlic, for example, served on a pistachio rice pilaf. But it's the simple food here that really shines.

The day we went for lunch, Chris had bought a beautiful snapper at his fishmonger, and with a minimum of fuss had grilled it over thinly sliced potato and seasoned it with herbs and a dressing of olive oil and lemon. We drank with it a Dalwhinnie chardonnay — Dalwhinnie winemaker David Jones is a mate of Chris's and a regular diner here — taken from a short but high quality list. (Yes, you're right, Dalwhinnie is from the Pyrenees, which is hardly what you'd describe as a local wine region, but it fits with the approach here: Chris sees his restaurant less as a great regional place and more of a great restaurant, full stop).

Dessert was just a large slice of lemon tart. ('The most beautiful lemon tart in Australia,' claims Chris. 'And if anybody says theirs is better, I'll cut off my finger.' It is a great lemon tart.)

That food all sounds so easy, doesn't it? And it was, but it was also one of the most wonderful meals I had researching this book. Often, the simplest things are not only the hardest to achieve, but can also be the most impressive.

This is a deceptively simple restaurant in many ways. Simply furnished, sensibly relying on its position for decorative value, and with some echoes of the straightforward Greek taverna (including slightly cheesy bazouki music), it nonetheless exudes hospitality, charm, professionalism and quality.

The most important element, of course, in Chris's success is Chris himself, and the packed years of experience he brings to the place.

Chris Talihmanidis started work in his aunt's restaurant on Salonika when he was thirteen. It wasn't long before he took it over, but he had his sights set on a wider world and decided to travel across Europe.

In 1960 he arrived in Australia and worked at Mount Buffalo, learning all the English words he needed to know, cooking breakfast for 180 people almost single-handed.

Melbourne followed: hotels, cafeterias, even a stint at Florentino followed by a short-lived bistro of his own. Greece beckoned and he went back, opening a small restaurant and getting involved with the Greek tourist board.

Above • Chris's famous lemon tart. Right • Chris Talihmanidis.

But Mr Talihmanidis obviously had the travel bug, because by 1965 he was back in Melbourne.

Then the fat finger of foodie fate decided to point Chris in a new direction. He saw a restaurant in Lorne for sale, the Marine Cafe, and decided to give it a go. The rest, as they say.... He stayed at the Marine for fourteen years, met his current partner, Penny, there, and forged a name for good Greek food and hospitality — teaching Aussie holiday makers that eating outside is fun, and teaching Aussie fisherfolk that calamari has other uses than being good bait.

Chris found and bought the property at Beacon Point in 1975. From the beginning, the accolades started coming in: one wall of the restaurant is plastered with yellowing articles of praise — including one written by Robert Morley, of all people. In 1992 the accommodation went in, and the package was complete. It is advisable to make bookings for both the villas and the restaurant (on a Friday or Saturday night particularly) months in advance.

Two years ago, the Talihmanidis empire expanded down the precipitous hill into Apollo Bay, when Penny opened the Sea Grape Wine Bar and Cafe on the main drag in town. Other very smart, city-savvy places have since opened (notably La Bimba, a bright and funky place that looks like it should be in Greville Street or Flinders Lane in Melbourne), but at the time, the Sea Grape was way ahead of the pack. With its modern food, solid, well-priced wine list and breezy, open spaces, it is still the best of them.

So, what next for Chris Talihmanidis? I asked him this as we finished our glasses of wine and polished off the schnapper. Perhaps he was just playing it up for the writer and photographer, but he talked of a book — and made big promises to Simon of trips to Greece, of great meals and wine: 'It will be a book not just of cooking, but of philosophy, a little biography, a little feelings.' And he rushed off to get an old picture book about Greece.

He finally found the image he was searching for and showed it to us: a haunting photograph of a hungry mother, gaunt, in black gowns. He stared at it for a few seconds and then put the book away.

'Now boys, who would like a little more wine?'

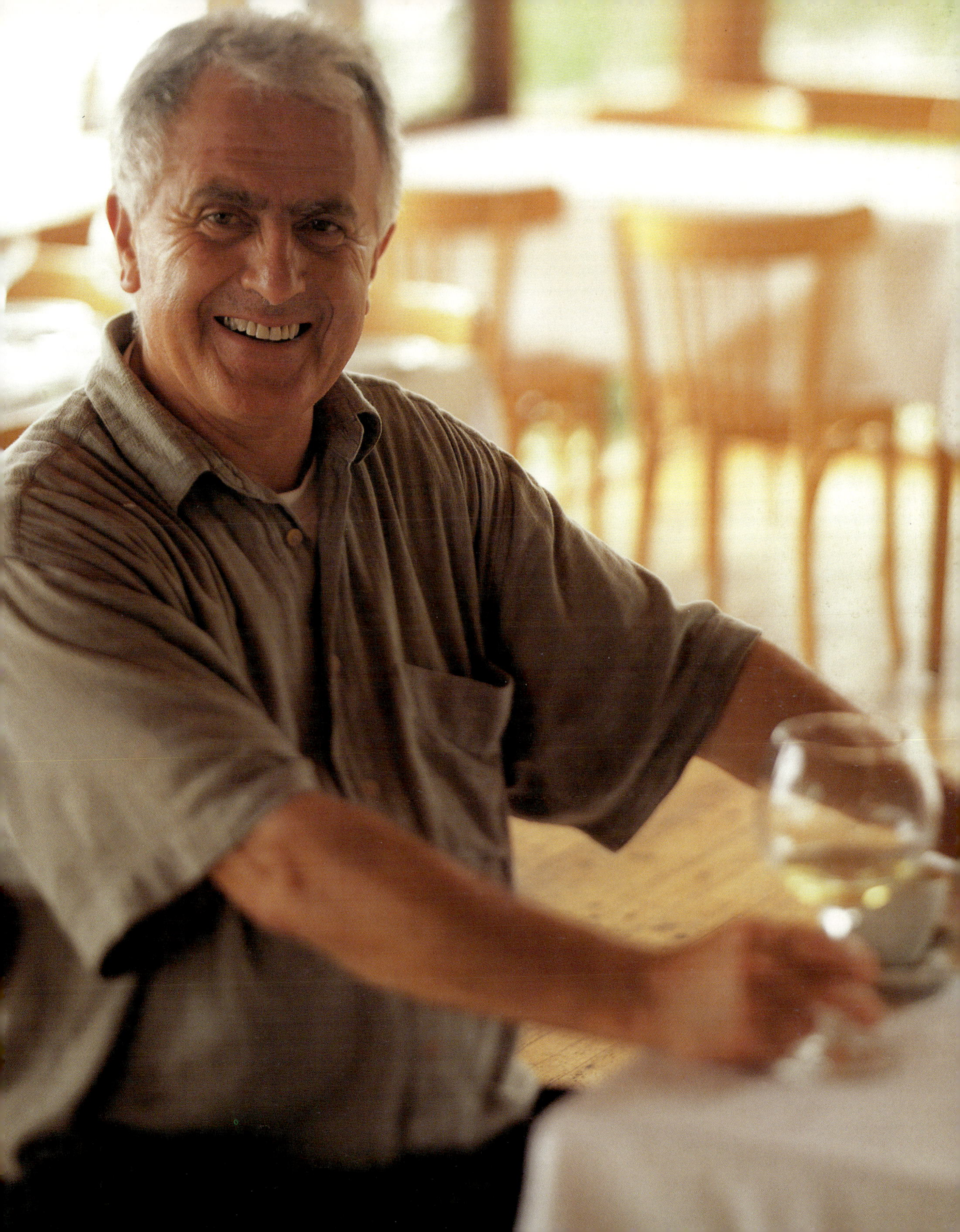

Port Fairy

I could live in Port Fairy. I could live there for a start because of the relaxed and welcoming Irish feel and hospitality. This old whaling village that straddles the wide River Moyne was known as Belfast for the first few years of its rugged life — today, still, there are B&Bs called Dublin House and Kilkarlen at Killarney. As you hurtle in on the road from Warrnambool past cottages of ever-increasing decrepitude you almost expect the Port Fairy welcome sign to say *cead mile failte* instead of plain old 'welcome'.

I could also live there because over the Labour Day weekend in late summer each year, the town is inundated by thousands of musos, hippies, travellers, yuppies, mums and dads and kids and dogs all down for the fabulous and famous Port Fairy Folk Festival. The *craic*, as they say, is mighty.

But most of all, I could live in Port Fairy because the people of Port Fairy eat well. The Merrijig Inn, for example, an ancient and particularly cute early settler hotel established in the 1840s, and The Stag, a bigger, decidedly more British-looking pub, both serve good, modern Australian food, packed with fresh produce, flecked here and there with the odd Asian influence. And then there is Lunch, arguably Port Fairy's best grubbery. Or it was.

As we go to press on the second edition of this book, it seems that Lunch has been sold. It remains to be seen what the new owners will do with the premises on Bank Street which have, in previous incarnations, been a post office and Port Fairy's council offices.

10 great picnic spots along the great ocean road

Botanic Gardens, Geelong

Paradise, Apollo Bay

Stephensons Falls, near Barramunga

Marriners Lookout, Apollo Bay

Blanket Bay, Otway National Park

Red Rock, Colac

Aire Crossing, Lavers Hill

The Redwoods, near Beech Forrest

Lake Elizabeth, near Forrest

Melba Gully, near Lavers Hill

VALENTINES DAY !
LOCAL CRAYFISH Available
with your choice of sauce
LIMITED NUMBERS...
The Stag
Entrance
Reception
from 6:30
(055)
1077

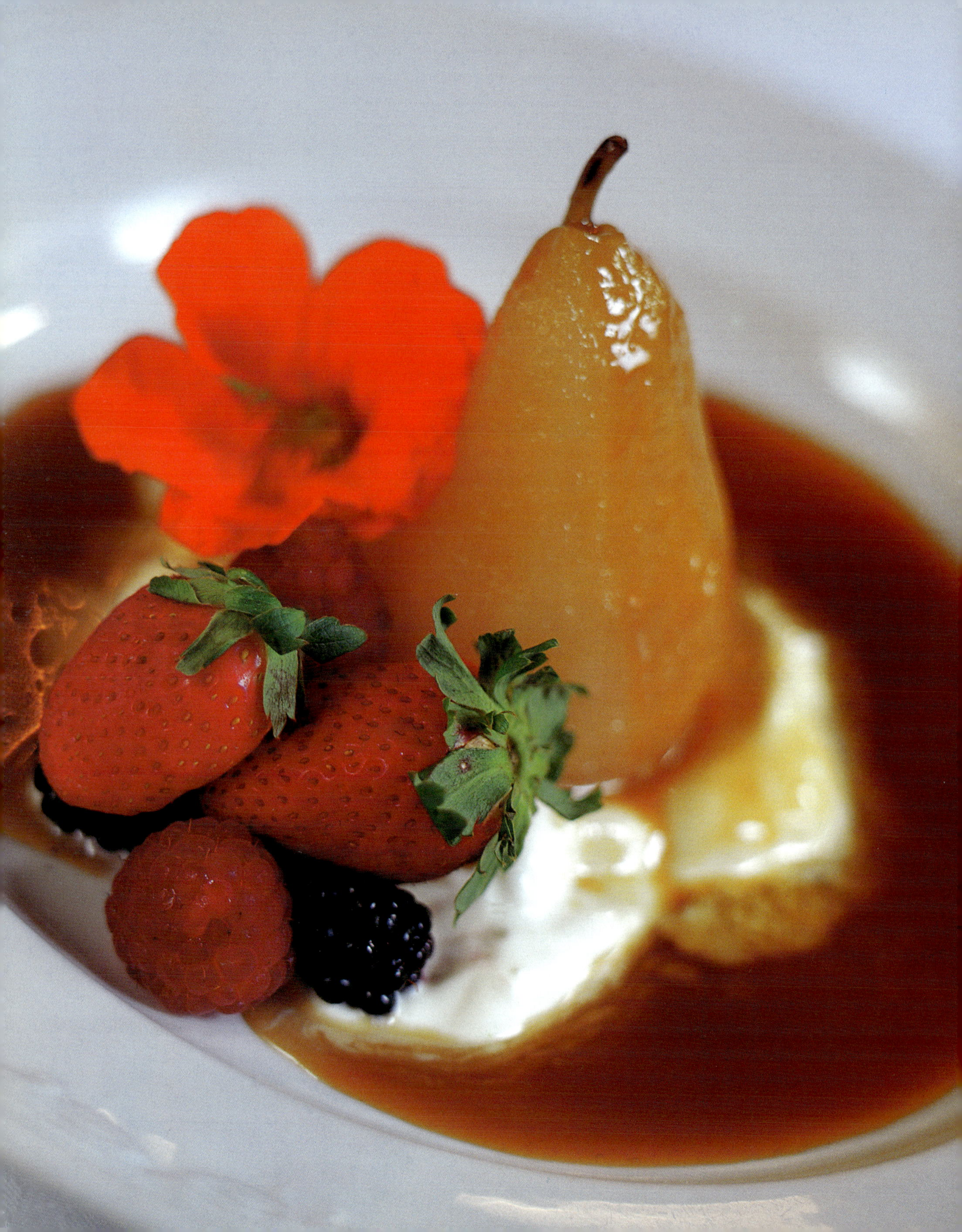

At the Restaurant

Local Scallops with Eggplant Cannelloni

Baked Polenta and Field Mushroom
Gratin with Timboon Blue

Veal Cutlet in an Envelope with
Roasted Vegetables and Red Wine Butter

Poached Corella Pears with Mascarpone
Cheese and Orange Caramel Sauce

Local Scallops with Eggplant Cannelloni

Fishermen's Pier, Geelong

Serves 4

100 ml olive oil

green herbs — 10 g each of basil, parsley, oregano, and thyme

24 fresh 'dry' scallops

sea salt and pepper

12 roasted eggplant slices

6 roasted red capsicum, de-seeded and skinned

150 g rocket

Infuse the olive oil with the green herbs by warming the oil and letting the herbs flavour the oil. Leave for at least an hour. Strain. This can be done the day before.

Pan sear the scallops very quickly, being careful not to over cook.

Toss the scallops in the herb-infused oil. Season, then wrap 2 scallops in each warmed eggplant slice.

Place 3 'cannelloni' over the warmed sliced capsicum, top with the rocket and serve.

Baked Polenta and Field Mushroom Gratin with Timboon Blue

Mark's Restaurant, Lorne

Serves 8

Polenta

800-1000 ml cold water

125 g unsalted butter

250 ml thickened cream

375 g polenta meal

salt and pepper

Bring water, butter and cream to boil. Slowly add polenta meal and cook until no longer gritty, stirring frequently. Add salt and pepper to taste.

In each gratin dish put 1 cm of hot polenta. Smooth and cover the base of the dish.

Mushrooms

100 g unsalted butter

100 ml good olive oil

2 large brown onions — finely chopped

1 kg cleaned field mushrooms, roughly chopped

salt and pepper

Melt butter, add oil and saute onions until transparent. Add mushrooms and cook until very tender. Puree in food processor. Add salt and pepper. Cool.

Cheese

300 g Timboon Blue (or any soft blue cheese)

300 g fresh cream cheese

Blend cheeses in food processor until well mixed.

To assemble

On top of the polenta base, fill the gratin dishes with 1 cm of mushroom puree, then the cheese mix randomly dolloped on the mushroom layer. You should see the mushrooms through the cheese mix.

Bake in a pre-heated 220°C oven for approximately 10 minutes or until the cheese is brown and molten.

Veal Cutlet in an Envelope with Roast Vegetables and Red Wine Butter

Mietta's Queenscliff Hotel, Queenscliff

Serves 4.

4 veal cutlets, trimmed with short bones (150-200 g)

salt and pepper

250 g butter — keep 150 g for sauce

1 cup chicken stock

2 turnips, cut into segments

1 celeriac, cut into large batons

1 carrot, cut into julienne

1 leek, cut into julienne

1 onion, cut into julienne

4 button mushrooms, finely sliced

julienne of zest from ¼ lemon

4 large sprigs thyme

4 bay leaves — small, fresh only

100 ml red wine (light in style)

1 dsp chopped shallots

4 x 30 cm circles of greaseproof paper

Season veal cutlets and lightly brown in butter. Boil chicken stock and blanch turnips and celeriac for 1 ½ minutes. Refresh under cold water.

Lay the greaseproof paper out and liberally brush with melted butter.

Mix carrot, leek and onion julienne together and divide equally on to the bottom half of the buttered greaseproof leaving at least 2.5 cm clear around the edges, then lay over the button mushrooms.

Place a veal cutlet on top, then neatly arrange the turnip, celeriac, lemon zest and herbs over the top. Fold the top half of the greaseproof over the top and twist the edges of the paper back on themselves to make an air tight seal.

Heat the oven to 200°C. In a small pot reduce the red wine and shallots to almost nothing and then set aside.

Place the veal papillotes onto a tray in the oven; they should take about 10-15 minutes to cook — they will puff up in the balloons if they have been properly sealed. Bring the red wine back to the boil and whisk in the butter to form a sauce, place in a jug to serve at the table.

Place the papillotes on warm plates and then in front of your guests slice the top of the balloons open with a very sharp knife.

Poached Corella Pears with Mascarpone Cheese and Orange Caramel Sauce

The Ozone Hotel, Queenscliff

Serves 6

Pears

6 Corella pears (any firm but ripe pear may be substituted)

1 medium rhizome fresh ginger, grated

2 stalks fresh lemon grass, roughly chopped

4 cinnamon sticks

2 cups port

sugar syrup

Peel pears and cut bases off so they sit flat. Stand pears in a heavy-based saucepan and add dry ingredients.

Add port and enough sugar syrup to cover and simmer over a low heat until pears are tender, approximately 40 minutes.

For extra flavour and colour, marinate pears in the poaching liquid for 24 hours before poaching.

Orange Caramel Sauce

200 g sugar

1 cup orange juice (no pulp)

100 ml water

500 ml double cream

Place sugar and water in a pan, bring to the boil and cook to a golden brown colour (175°C on the sugar thermometer). Remove from heat immediately and allow to cool a little.

Carefully pour in orange juice (it will spit hot caramel at you, so watch out!) and stir. Pour in double cream and return the mixture slowly to the boil, stirring occasionally.

To assemble

Pool sauce on the plate and place pear in the centre. Add a quenelle of mascarpone. Dust with a little powdered cinnamon

GEELONG & THE BELLARINE

Accommodation

OZONE HOTEL
42 Gellibrand St,
Queenscliff Vic 3225
Tel: 03 5258 1011
Fax: 03 5258 3712
Web: www.ozonehotel.com.au
Email: info@ozonehotel.com.au

Built in 1881, the Ozone Hotel radiates the warmth and character of turn-of-the-century charm and style. The 20 guest rooms all have bathrooms and are furnished with antique furniture, with some offering bay views. Some concessions to modern living include televisions and direct dial telephones. The restaurant creates fine contemporary food and offers a brilliant wine list.

THE VUE GRAND HOTEL
46 Hesse St,
Queenscliff Vic 3225
Tel: 03 5258 1544
Fax: 03 5258 3471
Email: info@vuegrand.com.au

There are 32 guest rooms with an appealing mix of accommodation – standard, balcony and spa rooms. All offer excellent facilities with traditional furnishings, creating a distinctive olde world charm. You can also discover a heated indoor swimming pool, spa and gym open 24 hours. Midweek and weekend packages available.

THE QUEENCLIFF HOTEL (MIETTA'S)
16 Gellibrand St,
Queenscliff Vic 3225
Tel: 03 5258 1066
Fax: 03 5258 1899
Email: enquiries@queenscliffhotel.com.au

The Queenscliff Hotel has the ambience of a large and beautifully restored and furnished 19th century country house, with open fires, drawing rooms, verandahs and gardens. All tariffs include breakfast and either lunch or dinner. Breakfast is a lavish meal, served on marble topped tables in a charming courtyard situation overlooking a pretty garden, or in the garden if weather permits, as is lunch. Dinner is served in the formal dining room with rose pink walls, gleaming silver, white linen, an open fire and candlelight, palms and flowers.

Restaurants & Cafes

ZEN ARTISAN CAFE BAKERY
153 High St,
Belmont Vic 3216
Tel: 03 5244 1488
Fax: 03 5244 2864

Located en route to the Surf Coast and Otway Ranges. Traditional continental and gourmet breads, cakes, coffee and lunch menu. It's the perfect place to stop, rest and pick up all your picnic needs for that trip to the beaches and forests of the west coast. Try our famous Pastadura.

CAFE BOTTICELLI
9/111 Pakington St,
Geelong West Vic 3218
Tel: 03 5229 8292
Fax: 03 5229 7699

Mediterranean.

FISHERMEN'S PIER
Bay End Yarra St,
Geelong Vic 3220
Tel: 03 5222 4100
Fax: 03 5223 2756
Web: www.fishermenspier.com.au
Email: info@fishermenspier.com.au

Geelong's unique seafood waterfront restaurant. Enjoy superb seafood and other dishes in a unique atmosphere. Situated on the water, with great views overlooking Corio Bay. A must when you visit the region or before driving down the Great Ocean Road. Fishermen's Pier is fully licensed, with over 40 varieties of local wines, and prides itself on using only the freshest and best seafood. Main menu changes daily. A real family atmosphere with children's menu. New alfresco dining area available. Three times winner of the American Express Gold Plate Award. Open seven days a week, lunch and dinner. 'You'll come for the food...you'll come back for the food.'

MIETTA'S QUEENCLIFF HOTEL
16 Gellibrand St,
Queenscliff Vic 3225
Tel: 03 5258 1066
Fax: 03 5258 1899
Email: enquiries@queenscliffhotel.com.au

Mietta's Queenscliff offers quality dining in the atmosphere of a large and beautifully restored 19th century country house with open fires, sitting rooms, verandahs and garden. Located in a unique Victorian era resort town only $1^1/_2$ hours from Melbourne. An ideal start or finish to a trip down the Great Ocean Road. Professional service, exceptional food and a wine list featuring the best of the Port Phillip region's wines make this a truly 5 star experience.

OZONE HOTEL
42 Gellibrand St,
Queenscliff Vic 3225
Tel: 03 5258 1011
Fax: 03 5258 3712
Web: www.ozonehotel.com.au
Email: info@ozonehotel.com.au

Built in 1881 in the grand Victorian style, the stately Ozone Hotel provides a choice of dining in either the Bistro & Garden Courtyard or the Grand Dining Room for a more formal occasion. A modern style of cuisine with a regional focus offers interesting contemporary food. Our award winning wine-list complements the food to give a sense of occasion to the dining experience.

SEMPRE CAFFE E PANINOTECA
88 Lt Mallop St, Geelong
Vic 3225
Tel: 03 5229 8845
Fax: 03 5229 8845

Italian.

THE VUE GRAND HOTEL
46 Hesse St,
Queenscliff Vic 3225
Tel: 03 5258 1544
Fax: 03 5258 3471
Email: info@vuegrand.com.au

Enjoy the Grand Dining Room and Outdoor Courtyards. Nowhere is the Vue Grand's well-preserved late Victorian splendour better reflected than in the Grand Dining Room. Regularly awarded two chef's hats in The Age Good Food Guide *for its cuisine and an admirable wine cellar to match. A la carte menu served for lunch and dinner, plus a seasonal two-course set menu including a glass of wine, tea/coffee at $19.99 per person, lunch only.*

WHOLEFOODS CAFE & GALLERY
10 James St,
Geelong Vic 3220
Tel: 03 5229 3909
Fax: 03 5229 3909

Delightful venue in the older, central arts and cafe precinct of Geelong city. Serving really good modern wholefood (nutritious gourmet) from local, seasonal and organic ingredients. Excellent pastries, seriously good Genovese coffee, T2 teas and expertly made authentic sourdough breads, baguettes and brioche. Fully licensed with a range of quality organic wines.

Produce

V&R FRUIT AND VEGETABLE MARKET
5 Pakington St,
West Geelong Vic 3218
Tel: 03 5222 2522
Fax: 03 5222 2515

V&R is loaded with fresh fruit and vegetables as well as an interesting range of local and imported cheeses, olive oils, breads and gourmet delicacies to tempt! Winner 1998 Melbourne Markets Certificate of Excellence and finalist in the Retailer of the Year 1998. The perfect place to stock-up on all your picnic provisions.

Wineries

KALINDA TOURS
PO Box 99,
Winchelsea Vic 3241
Tel: 03 5267 2581
Fax: 03 5267 2581

Wine-touring.

SURF COAST TO LORNE

Accommodation

ANGLESEA HISTORIC COTTAGE "SEA 'DRIFT"
c/o RSD H793
Ballarat Vic 3352
Tel: 03 5332 2644
Email: jcorb@netconnect.com.au
Web: www.netconnect.com.au/~jcorb

Old-world ambience c. 1917. Fully self-contained including quality linen, towels, cottage antiques. Wide verandah, wood-fire, aero-spa. North-facing courtyard. Exclusive Harvey Street frontage. Fantastic location opposite reserve 500 metres from beach, river, café. Dine (in or out.) Hear the sea, watch the sunrise, walk in the coastal forest. Relax, unwind, enjoy.

BUSHLAND RETREAT
Luggs Rd,
Aireys Inlet Vic 3220
Tel: 03 5289 7245

A stylish but simple mudbrick house in the bush. Decorated with the owner's hand-made furniture and other local artists' mosaics, iron work and paintings. A spacious house with three bedrooms, two living areas, a large kitchen/diningroom, timber floors and wood burning fire.

BUSH TO BEACH BED & BREAKFAST
43 Anderson St,
Aireys Inlet Vic 3231
Tel: 03 5289 6538
Fax: 03 5289 6538
Web: www.tourvic.com.au
Email: bushtobeach@yahoo.com

Located in tranquil bush, only minutes from the sea, Bush to Beach offers a unique opportunity for you to experience Australian wildlife first-hand. Combine this with excellent country cooking, home-made breads, home-grown fruits, vegetables and eggs, and your stay is memorable. Nature tours and evening meals by arrangement.

CUMBERLAND LORNE RESORT
150-178 Mountjoy Pde,
Lorne Vic 3232
Tel: 03 5289 2400

Award Winning Excellence for 'Deluxe Accommodation'. Cumberland Lorne Resort is located on the spectacular Great Ocean Road in the heart of Lorne, a comfortable 1³/₄ hour drive from Melbourne. This 4¹/₂ star resort offers 99 luxuriously appointed suites, all with private balconies and spas. Award-winning purpose built conference centre, extensive recreational facilities and the fully licensed Chris's restaurant.

PHOENIX APARTMENTS
60 Mountjoy Pde,
Lorne Vic 3232
Tel: 0414 528 911
Fax: 03 5289 1298

Phoenix Apartments reflect Melbourne designer Chris Connell's love of surf, sun, sand and the simplicity of life on the beach. Elegant, modern, self-contained apartments feature spacious rooms with polished wood floors, individual balconies and gorgeous ocean views as well as fully equipped kitchens. Located in central Lorne – right across the road from the main beach. The apartments operate in conjunction with and are complemented by Kosta's Restaurant, famous for its fresh seafood and lively atmosphere. Weekend and mid-week packages are available. "...A fabulous little getaway that those in the know are keen to keep under wraps..." Belle Magazine, Feb 1998

Restaurants & Cafes

ANGLESEA OLIVE TREE CAFE
12/87 Great Ocean Rd,
Anglesea Vic 3230
Tel: 03 5263 1010

Modern.

CAFE FALLS
Erskine Falls Rd,
Lorne Vic 3232
Tel: 03 5289 2666
Fax: 03 5289 2247

Set halfway between Lorne and Erskine Falls, Cafe Falls is the perfect stop for morning or afternoon tea, or gourmet lunch. Enjoy scrumptious food and the beautiful coastline views. Hand feed the wild parrots of the surrounding State Forest. Open 8.30am – 5.00pm daily. Lunches, Devonshire teas and breakfast served all day.

CUMBERLAND LORNE RESORT
Chris's Lorne
150-178 Mountjoy Pde,
Lorne Vic 3232
Tel: 03 5289 2400

Chris's Restaurant and Bar offers great views across the magnificent foreshore. Featuring Contemporary International Cuisine, friendly service and a relaxed atmosphere, Chris's provides great al fresco dining. The restaurant is open throughout the year, serving everything from light meals to coffee and cake on the Terrace or a spectacular three-course dinner.

HEATHLANDS TEA HOUSE & GALLERY
243 Great Ocean Road,
Anglesea Vic 3230
Tel: 03 5263 3471
Fax: 03 5263 3558

The Teahouse & Gallery overlook picturesque gardens with sea views to Airey's Inlet and beyond. Enjoy our Devonshire Teas with home-made jams, King Island cream, light lunches and daily special. Relax on the verandah, air-conditioned comfort or cosy fire. Featuring local art work, gifts and souvenirs. Situated 3.5kms Lorne side of Anglesea.

LORNE HOTEL
176 Mountjoy Pde,
Lorne Vic 3232
Tel: 03 5289 1409
Fax: 03 5289 2200

Our ocean view bistro offers an extensive menu, from light snacks, coffee and cakes to chargrilled steaks and function menus. Local seafood specials feature daily and a special 'nippers' menu for the children. Accommodation; pub; TAB; beer garden; ocean views; Sky Channel; live entertainment.

LORNE OVENHOUSE
46a Mountjoy Pde,
Lorne Vic 3232
Tel: 03 5289 2544
Fax: 03 5289 2544

Located in the heart of Lorne, with the family in mind, the Ovenhouse offers a substantial children's menu & quality adult selections. Wood fired gourmet pizza, pastas, steaks, seafood and salads. Fully licensed with a wide range of desserts and coffee, the Ovenhouse is a great stop for that quick bite or leisurely dinner.

MARINE CAFE
6a Mountjoy Pde,
Lorne Vic 3232
Tel: 03 5289 1808
Fax: 03 5289 1707

Delectable.

MARK'S RESTAURANT
124 Mountjoy Pde,
Lorne Vic 3232
Tel: 03 5289 2787
Fax: 03 5289 2787

Sleek, smart and spacious – Mark's has a modern sensibility that extends from mood all the way through to the seasonal menu. The emphasis lies on fresh seafood and local produce. Come to savour great ocean views, seriously good food and a wine list boasting Australia's best. Open for lunch Saturday & Sunday 12-3pm, and every night from 6pm for fine dining.

TIRAMI-SU ITALIAN RESTAURANT
1a Grove Rd,
Lorne Vic 3232
Tel: 03 5289 1004
Email: tiramisu@primus.com.au

Authentic Italian food with singing chef Alfonso Rinaldi. Open daily for lunch 12-3.30pm and dinner 6pm till late. Run by husband and wife team Ditta and Alfonso both with extensive European experience. Fully licensed. Bookings recommended.

STICKY FINGERS
2/4 Gilbert St,
Airey's Inlet Vic 3220
Tel: 03 5289 6645

Freshly made food and great espresso coffee to enjoy in a real bush setting. A variety of pure honey and condiments; sour dough bread, yummy cakes, scrolls, muffins, biscuits all baked on-site; vegetarian and meat-lover's delight; range of giftware; food intolerances catered for. Open: Fri, Sat, Sun – 9am-5pm (7 days over summer and school holidays).

APOLLO BAY & THE OTWAYS

Accommodation

CLAERWEN RETREAT
Tuxion Rd,
Apollo Bay Vic 3233
Tel: 03 5237 7064
Fax: 03 5237 7054
Web: www.claerwen.com.au
Email: cornelia_elbrecht@claerwen.com.au

Luxurious country guest-house. Spacious rooms with en-suite. Huge lounge, library, dining area. Three bedroom holiday houses with open fire, salt water pool, hot spa and tennis court. 130 acres of park, bush and fern gullies. Overlooking the coast with panoramic views from all rooms. RACV rating 4½ stars.

ELLIMINOOK HOMESTEAD
'Elliminook', Birregurra Vic 3242
Tel: 03 5236 2080
Fax: 03 5236 2423
Email: inquiries@elliminook.com.au
Website: www.elliminook.com.au

This beautifully restored National Trust classified 1865 homestead is set in a historic garden with a tennis court and croquet lawn. Enjoy fresh flowers, cosy fires, indulgent breakfasts, antique furnishings, guest sitting room and elegant ensuite bedrooms. 'Elliminook' is located at Birregurra, only five minutes drive from Sunnybrae restaurant.

FORREST COUNTRY GUESTHOUSE & RESTAURANT
Main Rd,
Forrest Vic 3236
Tel: 03 5236 6446
Fax: 03 5236 6446

Swiss-style.

TARNDWARNCOORT COTTAGE
Tarndwarncoort,
Warncoort Vic 3243
Tel: 03 5233 6241
Fax: 03 5233 6338
Email: wendydennis@primus.com.au

Self-contained.

WHITE CREST OCEAN-SIDE RESORT
PO Box 148,
Apollo Bay Vic 3233
Tel: 03 5237 0228
Fax: 03 5237 0245

See our entry under Restaurants & Cafés.

Restaurants & Cafes

BEACHES RESTAURANT & BAR
cnr Great Ocean Rd & Nelson St,
Apollo Bay Vic 3233
Tel: 03 5237 6309
Fax: 03 5237 6891
Email: greenacres@vicnet.net.au

Modern Australian/Seafood. Beaches at Greenacres Country House boasts good food, good wine and great views over the golf course, ocean and Otway Ranges. Idyllic spot for lunch or dinner to soak up the fishing village atmosphere, either at a sunny window table or a candle-lit table by the fire when it's wild and wintry.

PISCES ON THE PARK
Great Ocean Rd,
Apollo Bay Vic 3233
Tel: 03 5237 7118
Fax: 03 5237 7252

Seafood.

WHITE CREST OCEAN-SIDE RESORT
PO Box 148,
Apollo Bay Vic 3233
Tel: 03 5237 0228
Fax: 03 5237 0245

Situated on the rugged coastline of the Great Ocean Road, just metres above the ocean, diners at White Crest enjoy unsurpassed rural and sea views. The menu, which changes seasonally, emphasises well prepared and presented fresh local produce including seafood and crayfish, when available. On winter evenings, the open log fire adds to the warm and comfortable ambience. White Crest also offers a secluded retreat for those in need of a tranquil break. Its 10 comfortable split-level apartments all have ocean views, cosy open fires, bathroom, kitchenette and private balconies.

COLAC, CAMPERDOWN AND COBDEN

Restaurants & Cafes

LIZZIES ON MANIFOLD
153 Manifold St,
Camperdown Vic 3260
Tel: 03 5593 1336

Modern.

Other

LEE'S IGA SUPERMARKETS
139 Manifold St,
Camperdown Vic 3260
Tel: 03 5593 1744
Cobden: 03 5595 1017
Timboon: 03 5598 3013

SHIPWRECK COAST TO THE BORDER

Accommodation

PORT FAIRY COLONIAL COTTAGES
PO Box 50,
Port Fairy Vic 3782
Tel: 03 5568 1234
Fax: 03 5568 2966
Email: cottages@ansonic.com.au

Two lovingly restored colonial cottages – one 1856 stone, the other an 1880's timber cottage – centrally located in historic Port Fairy close to the river, wharf, beach and restaurants. Delightfully decorated with brass beds, antiques and collectables. Featuring romantic bluestone fireplaces, colonial charm and atmosphere. Fully self-contained, including linen, fresh flowers, set in cottage gardens.

COTTAGES OF THE PORT
PO Box 192,
Port Fairy Vic 3284
Tel: 03 5568 7345
Fax: 03 5568 7345
Email: cottages@standard.net.au
Web: www.cottagesoftheport.com.au

Charming self-contained historic cottages in the heart of the picturesque village of Port Fairy, close to the river, beach and restaurants. Open fires, country style décor, antiques, books and fresh flowers for guests to enjoy. Gourmet breakfast provisions can be arranged for short visits.

Restaurants & Cafes

BALENAS
158 Timor St,
Warrnambool Vic 3280
Tel: 03 5562 0900
Fax: 03 5561 3893

Contemporary.

BLACK WATTLE MOTEL
Mt Gambier Road,
Nelson Vic 3292
Tel: 08 8738 4008
Fax: 08 8738 4292
Web: www.bwattle.mtx.net

Spectacular views over the Discovery Bay National Park, the Glenelg River and the Southern Ocean make for a fine wining and dining experience at Nelson. A comprehensive selection of local wines complement modern Australian cuisine featuring the best in local produce. Comfortable 3-star accommodation available in an off-road location.

FRESHWATER CAFE
78 Leibig St,
Warrnambool Vic 3280
Tel: 03 5561 3188
Fax: 03 5561 7238

Modern.

NAPIER'S RESTAURANT
1 Lord St,
Port Campbell Vic 3269
Tel: 03 5598 6231
Fax: 03 5598 6471
Email: tolloch@ansonic.com.au

Close to the Pier, overlooking the bay of Port Campbell, Napier's fully licensed restaurant specialises in Southern Rock Lobster and fresh local produce in season, such as Timboon Farmhouse Cheese, strawberries and regional wines.

THE STAG RESTAURANT AT SEACOMBE HOUSE
cnr Cox & Sackville Sts,
Port Fairy Vic 3284
Tel: 03 5568 1077
Fax: 03 5568 2323
Email: seacport@fc-hotels.com.au

Relaxed fine dining in National Trust classified surroundings established in 1847. A special treat for seafood lovers without excluding other preferences, including vegetarian. The Stag menu offers fine fresh produce from local and surrounding areas, using traditional cooking methods with a modern influence. Listed in The Age Good Food Guide and with an extensive award-winning range of local and overseas wines tucked away in bluestone cellars.

Looking for somewhere to stay? Seacombe House has it all. From historical budget B&B to modern 3^1/$_2$ star units and National Trust cottages with open fires and double spas. Enquiries: 03 5568 1082

Recipe index

abalone 44
Angel's Jamon with Fresh Figs 48
Artichoke and Potato Galette 110

Baked Polenta and Field Mushroom
   Gratin with Timboon Blue
   Cheese 132-3
blue cheese
   Baked Polenta and Field Mushroom
      Gratin with Timboon Blue
      Cheese 132-3
Butter Beans with Pork 92

cake
   Cous Cous Fruitcake with Orange
      Blossom Water and Pistachio 69
cannelloni
   Local Scallops with Eggplant
      Cannelloni 132
capers
   Portarlington Mussels with Red
      Pepper and Capers 48
chicken
   Screaming Chicken 49
Chris's Kakavia Greek Seafood
   Soup 68
Cous Cous Fruitcake with Orange
   Blossom Water and Pistachio 69
crab
   Gâteau of King Crab and
      Scallops 108-9
crayfish 40

dessert
   Passionfruit Brûlée Tart with Ginger
      Cream, Warm Compote of Berries
      and a Poppyseed Wafer 111
   Poached Corella Pears with
      Mascarpone Cheese and Orange
      Caramel Sauce 133
   Quince Puddings with Vanilla
      Custard and a Quince Syrup 93
   Raspberry Citrus Tart with Ricotta 49
Duck with Aperol, Pear and Wild
   Rocket 109

eel
   Vine-ripened Tomato Consomme
      with Quenelles of Eel 108
eggplant
   Local Scallops with Eggplant
      Cannelloni 132

figs
   Angel's Jamon with Fresh Figs 48
Fricassee of Meredith Milk-fed
   Lamb 69
Gâteau of King Crab and
   Scallops 108-9
globe artichoke 44
Greek Egg and Lemon Soup 93
Greek Seafood Soup,
   Chris's Kakavian 68
Grilled Vegetable and Purrumbete
   Mozzarella Tart 92

jamon
   Angel's Jamon with Fresh Figs 48

Lamb, Fricassee of Meredith
   Milk-fed 69
leeks
   Small Leeks braised in Pinot 49
lemon
   Greek Egg and Lemon Soup 93
Local Scallops with Eggplant
   Cannelloni 132

mascarpone cheese
   Poached Corella Pears with
      Mascarpone Cheese and Orange
      Caramel Sauce 133
Meredith Blue with Poppyseed
   Carackers 49
Mt Elephant Pecorino Tart with
   Provençale Paste 68
mozzarella cheese
   Shaw River Mozzarella and
      Grilled Vegetable Tart 92
mushrooms
   Baked Polenta and Field
      Mushroom Gratin with Timboon
      Blue Cheese 132-3
mussels
   Portarlington Mussels with Red
      Pepper and Capers 48

Passionfruit Brûlée Tart with Ginger
   Cream, Warm Compote of Berries
   and a Poppyseed Wafer 111
pears
   Duck with Aperol, Pear & Wild
      Rocket 109
   Poached Corella Pears with
      Mascarpone Cheese and Orange
      Caramel Sauce 137
Pecorino Tart with Provencale Paste 68
Pistachio: Cous Cous Fruitcake with
   Orange Blossom Water and 69

Poached Corella Pears with
   Mascarpone Cheese and Orange
   Caramel Sauce 133

polenta
   Baked Polenta and Field
      Mushroom Gratin with Timboon
      Blue Cheese 132-3
Pork with Butter Beans 92
Portarlington Mussels with Red
   Pepper and Capers 48
Potato and Artichoke Galette 110
Provençale Paste 68

Quince Puddings with Vanilla Custard
   and a Quince Syrup 93

Raspberry Citrus Tart with Ricotta 49
red peppers
   Portarlington Mussels with Red
      Pepper and Capers 48
Ricotta with Raspberry Citrus Tart 49

scallops
   Gâteau of King Crab and
      Scallops 108-9
   Local Scallops with Eggplant
      Cannelloni 136
Screaming Chicken 49
Small Leeks braised in Pinot 49
Sourdough Starter 37
soup
   Chris's Kakavia Greek Seafood
      Soup 68
   Greek Egg and Lemon Soup 93
   Vine-ripened Tomato Consomme
      with Quenelles of Eel 108

tarts
   Grilled Vegetable and Shaw River
      Mozzarella 92
   Mt Elephant Pecorino Tart with
      Provençale Paste 68
   Passionfruit Brûlée Tart with Ginger
      Cream, Warm Compote of Berries
      and a Poppyseed Wafer 111
   Raspberry Citrus Tart with Ricotta 49
tomato
   Vine-ripened Tomato Consomme
      with Quenelles of Eel 108

Veal Cutlet in an Envelope with Roast
   Vegetables and Red Wine Butter 133
Vine-ripened Tomato Consomme with
   Quenelles of Eel 108

Index

abalone 43-4
Aire Crossing (Lavers Hill) 132
Aireys Inlet 38, 84, 135, 136
Allenvale Cottages (Lorne) 104
Anglesea Historic Cottage
 "Sea 'Drift" 135
Anglesea Olive Tree Cafe 136
Angus, Graham and Charlene 38-40
Apollo Bay 41-3, 114, 128, 137

bacon 40
Baillieu, George 100
Balenas 138
Bannockburn Cellars 80
Bannockburn Vineyards 75-8
Barrabool and Waybourne Winery 73
Barongavale 73
Barwon Seafoods 93
Bazil's Foodstore 48
Beaches Restaurant & Bar 133
Beech Forest 124
beer 84
Bellman, Alan 40
berries 45
biodynamics 53, 55
Biron, George 75
Birregurra 37-8
biscuits 36-7
Bitton, Phil 103
Blanket Bay (Otway National Park) 128
Bonlac 58, 63
Bons, Cornelius and Cornelia 45
Botanic Gardens (Geelong) 128
Browne, David 81
Brockett, Robin 83
buffalo 60-5
Bush to Beach Bed and
 Breakfast 104, 135
Bushland Retreat 135

Cachia, Albie 35, 36
Cafe Botticelli 48, 120, 134
Cafe Falls 136
Cafe Felix 117
Campbell, Ken and Joy 73
Camperdown 56, 57, 137
Cape Otway Cottages 104
Cardoso, Angel 29-31
cheese 52-65
Chris's Beacon Point Restaurant
 68, 114, 122, 125-26
Cindy's butchery 37-8
Claerwen Retreat 137
Clyde Park 73
Cobden Country-Style Smokehouse 40
Cocks, Sandy 127-8
coffee 117
Colac 73, 128
Cole, Chas 80
Corio Distillery 84
Cottages of the Port 138

Crawford River Vineyard 87-8
crayfish 40, 41-3
Cumberland Lorne Resort 135-6

Dark Horse 73
Davidson, Darryl 100
de Leo, Mary 117
Dickinson, David 127-8
Distillery Creek 84
Dixon, Peter 124
Drumborg 87-8

Elliminook (Birregurra) 104
Empire Grill 117

Farnan, John and Jan 119
Farr, Gary 73, 75-6, 78
Figaro's Deli and Coffee 117
fish 41-5
Fishermen's Pier 114, 132, 134
Fitzpatrick, Donlevy 73
Forrest 128, 137
Forrest Country Guesthouse
 & Restaurant 137
Freshwater Cafe 138
Freshwater Creek Cake Shop 33

Gangemi, Vince and Rosa 32
Geelong 72-3, 80, 84, 114, 117-20, 128
Geelong Winegrowers' Association 75
Gobles Millhouse (Port Fairy) 104
Goslin, Joseph 99
Graillot, Alain 78
Grimshaw, David 45
Guiseppes, Cafe 117

Haddow, Nick 63
Haldane, Roger and Sue 60-5
Harrop, Matt 73
Harry's 121
Heath, Greg 103
Heathlands Teahouse & Gallery 136
Hooper, Stuart 73, 75, 80
Hordern Vale House (Aire Valley) 104
Hradil, Vladimir 104
Hyett, Bruce 73, 79

Idyll Vineyard 72
Ireland, Scott 73

Kalinda Tours 135
Kilgour Estate 73
King Parrot (Pennyroyal) 104
Knox, Tony 99
Koch, Andrew 117
Kosta's 69, 114, 117, 122-3
Kraft 52

Lake Elizabeth (near Forrest) 128
Lake Purrumbete 56
Langtons Wine Auctions 73
Lavers Hill 128
le Grand, Stephane 104

Le Parisien 114
Leahy, Karin 36-7
Lee's IGA Supermarkets 137
Little, Rohan 73
Lizzies on Manifold 137
Living Organics 45
Lorne 114, 122-3, 135, 136
Lorne Ovenhouse 140
Lorne Hotel 140
Lunch 128

McGill, Gerard 36
Maltby, Tom 73
Manifold, Robert 57-60
Manifold, William 56
Marine Cafe 111, 136
Mark's Restaurant 132, 136
Marriners Lookout (Apollo Bay) 128
Melba Gully (near Lavers Hill) 128
Melbourne Wine Company 73
Mietta's Queenscliff Hotel 96-100, 117,
 133, 134
Moons Cafe 117
Morrison, George Ernest 'Chinese', 87
Motel Black Wattle 138
Mount Duneed Vinyard 73
Mount Emu Creek 56-60, 63
mushrooms 120

Napier's Restaurant 138
Neuschafers 80
Nelson 138
New Beginnings (Fairhaven) 104
Nugent, Martha 99

O'Donnell, Mietta 99
One 5 Three 117
organic farming/food 45, 55, 119
Otway Wines 73
Ozone Hotel 100-3, 133, 134

Paradise (Apollo Bay) 128
Pelikan brand butter 56
Pennyroyal Raspberry Farm
 (Pennyroyal) 104
Pettavel, David 73, 79
Phoenix Apartments 135
picnic spots 128
Pisces on the Park 137
Polgeest, Nick 41-3
Pollard, Randall 80
Pop Food Express 120
Port Campbell 138
Port Fairy 114, 126-8, 137-8
Port Fairy Colonial Cottages 137
Powell, Lindsay 120
Prince Albert Vineyard 73, 79, 118
Pud's Pantry and Deli 49
Purrumbete 60-5

Queenscliff 95-105, 121
Queenscliff Hotel 117, 134

Red Rock (Colac) 128
Red Rock Winery 73
Regal Ice Cream 52
Ritchie, Kelly 124

Sawyer's Arms Tavern 93
Schulz, Hermann 52-6
Scotchmans Hill Vineyard 73, 81-3
Screaming Seeds Spice Company
    35-6, 48
Sea Grape Wine Bar 114
Sefton, Daryl and Nini 72-3
Sempre Cafe 109, 117-18, 134
Seppelt, Karl 87-8
Shannon, Joel 43-4
sheep 57
Smits, Esther 36
Spray Farm 73, 83
spices 35-6
Staaks, John 58
Steam Packet Brewing Company 84
Stephensons Falls (near Barramunga) 128
Sticky Fingers 38-40, 136
Sunnybrae Country Restaurant
    48, 68, 110

Talihmanidis, Chris 122, 125-6
Talihmanidis, Kosta 122
Taranto, Chris 117
Tarndwarncoort Cottage 137
The Bay Leaf Cafe 117
The Biscuit Tin 36-7
The Redwoods (near Beech
    Forest) 128
The Rookery Nook Hotel 124
The Stag Restaurant at Seacombe
    House 138
Thomas, Gail 92, 114
Thomson, John and Cathy 87-8
Timboon 52-6
Tirami-su Italian Restaurant 136
Toussons 108

V&R Fruit and Vegetable Market 135
Vue Grand 103-4, 108, 134, 135

Waurn Ponds 72, 73
Warrnambool 52, 138
Warrnambool Butter and Cheese
    Factory 52
White, Dennis 45
White Crest Ocean-Side Resort 137
Wholefoods Cafe 69, 119, 135
wine 70-88, 135
Williams, Martin 73
Wollaston (Warrnambool) 104
Wye River 124

yoghurt 57-8, 63

Zambelli, Otto 73
Zen Artisan Cafe Bakery 134
Zen, Danny 33

References

Great Southern Food and Wine Guide, Tourism Victoria

Great Ocean Road – Second Edition, Rodney Hyett, Great Ocean Publications

Along the Great Ocean Road – The Local Pubs, Keith L. Cecil, Anglesea and District Historical Society

Along the Great Ocean Road – The Great Ocean Road, Keith L. Cecil, Anglesea and District Historical Society

A History of the Great Ocean Road, Peter Alsop, Geelong Historical Society

The Story of Geelong 1800 – 1990, N. Houghton, Geelong Historical Records Centre

The Otways that I Knew, Corker Brown, Self-Published

Victoria, Cream of the Country – A History of Victorian Dairying, Norman Godbold, Dairy Industry Association of Australia

From Boudry to the Barrabool Hills – The Swiss Vignerons of Geelong, John Tetaz, Australian Scholarly Publishing

Better than Pommard – A History of Wine in Victoria, David Dunstan, Australian Scholarly Publishing

Off the Plate – Restaurant and Catering Association Australia 1998 Conference Proceedings, RCAA

'A Road Less Travelled', article by Matthew Evans, *Australian Gourmet Traveller*, Jan 1998

Two stories told in this book originally appeared in quite different forms elsewhere:

The story on Mietta's Queenscliff Hotel is based on a restaurant review for *The Melbourne Weekly* magazine in January, 1999

The story on wine in the far south west of Victoria originally appeared as an article about Crawford River in *The Australian Magazine* in October 1998.

Credits

Photography • Simon Griffiths, except as follows:

Introduction
pages 14, 15, 17, 18, 19, 21 and 24
• Geelong Historical Records Society
page 20
• Image Library, State Library of NSW
page 24
• 'Surfari to Point Lonsdale', by Jack Eden.

From the earth to the table
page 40 • Sandy Scheltema

The cheesemakers
page 62-4 • Robert Ashton

Kitchens and cooks
page 114 • Sandy Scheltema

Map • Diana Platt

Index • Russell Brooks

142 + 16 = 158